Homesteads
and Snug Harbours

Contents

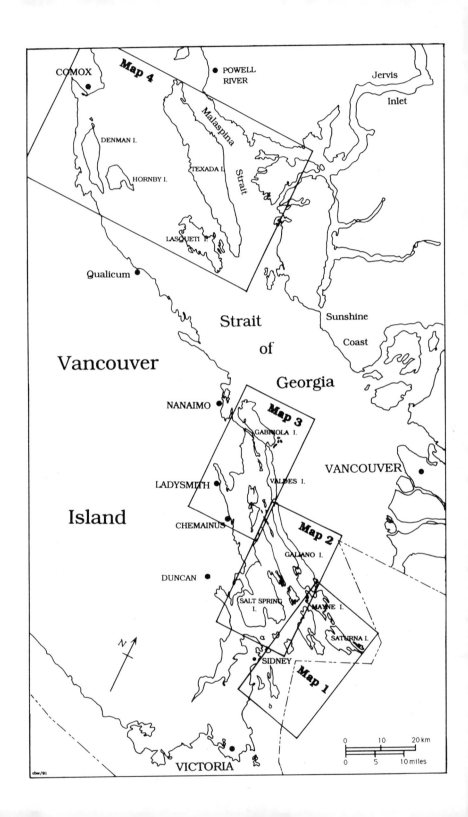

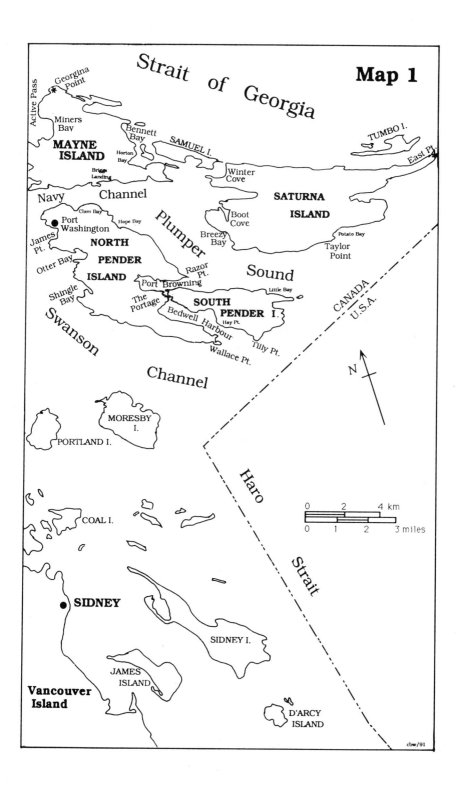

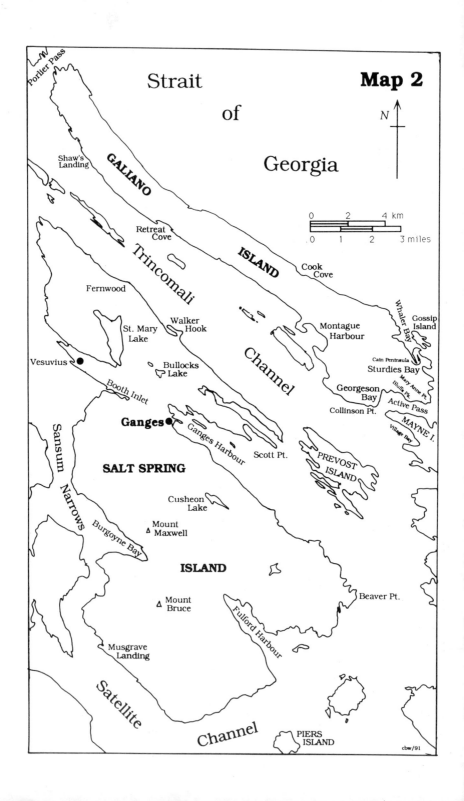

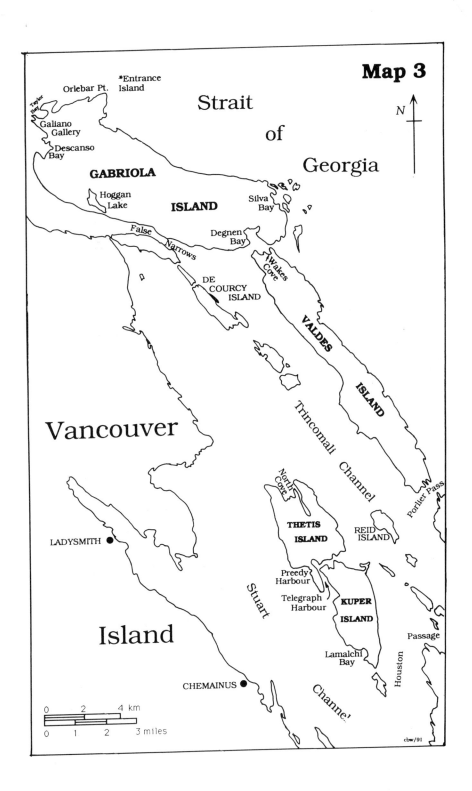

Map 3

N

Strait
of
Georgia

*Entrance Island
Orlebar Pt.
Taylor Bay
Galiano Gallery
Descanso Bay

GABRIOLA

Hoggan Lake

ISLAND

Silva Bay

False Narrows

Degnen Bay

Wakes Cove

DE COURCY ISLAND

VALDES

ISLAND

Trincomali Channel

Vancouver

Porlier Pass

North Cove

THETIS ISLAND

REID ISLAND

LADYSMITH ●

Preedy Harbour

Stuart

Telegraph Harbour

KUPER

ISLAND

Passage

Houston

Lamalchi Bay

Island

CHEMAINUS ●

Channel

0   2   4 km
0   1   2   3 miles

cbw/91

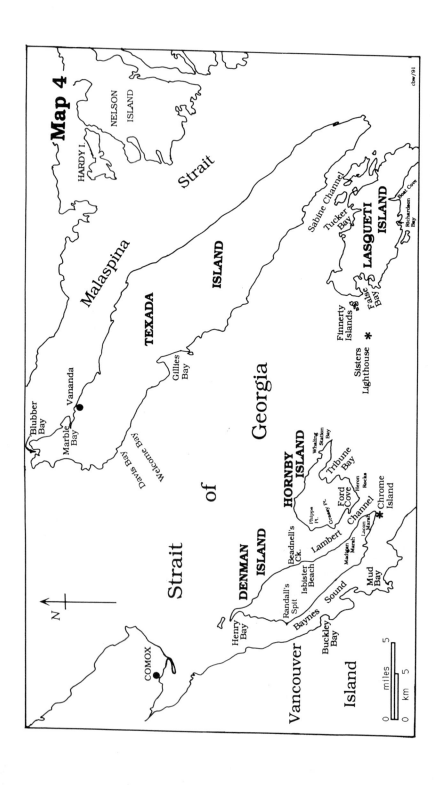

Map 4

NELSON ISLAND

HARDY I.

Malaspina Strait

TEXADA ISLAND

Blubber Bay

Vananda

Marble Bay

Davis Bay

Welcome Bay

Gillies Bay

Sabine Channel

Tucker Bay

LASQUETI ISLAND

Boat Cove

Richardson Bay

False Bay

Finnerty Islands

Sisters Lighthouse ✱

Strait of Georgia

DENMAN ISLAND

HORNBY ISLAND

Whaling Station Bay

Tribune Bay

Ford Cove

Heron Rocks

Phipps Pt.

Grassy Pt.

Chrome Island ✱

Lambert Channel

Beadnell's Ck.

Isbister Beach

Randall's Spit

Madigan Marsh

Lacon Marsh

Mud Bay

Henry Bay

Baynes Sound

Buckley Bay

COMOX

Vancouver Island

N

0   miles   5

0   km   5

cbw/91

Introduction

There's no question—the Gulf Islands *are* different, special places. Their uniqueness attracted the first settlers and continues to lure individualists, both young and old, seeking another way of life. "Island communities are the original alternative societies," John Fowles has written. "Of their nature they break down the multiple alienations of industrial and suburban man. Some vision of Utopian belonging, of social blessedness, of an independence based on co-operation, haunts them all."

The problem is, as any Gulf Islander will tell you as the ferry drops another load of automobiles on his doorstep, how do you maintain that way of life when more and more people want to share it? Jack Scott, a big-city newspaper columnist who managed to spend the best years of his life working and loafing on Salt Spring's Booth Bay, recognized the dilemma: "Like those early discoverers of gold on the Klondike who couldn't keep from babbling their secret, the Gulf Island discoverer of pay dirt seems incapable of keeping his big yap shut. He runs off in all directions hollering 'Gold! Gold!' and the rush is on."

Writing about his beloved Scilly Islands, John Fowles noted that "all the islands are under the protection of the Duchy of Cornwall and even more importantly, under that of a strong native disinclination (which makes them rare indeed these days) to give any ground to the dominant syllogism: profit is life, tourists bring profit, therefore let us sacrifice everything to tourism."

The Gulf Islanders don't have the Duchy of Cornwall protecting their interests, but since 1974 they have had the Islands Trust. A creature of the provincial government, the Trust declares its purpose "to preserve and protect, in co-operation with the municipalities and the Government of the Province, the Trust Area and its unique amenities and environment for the benefit of the residents of the Trust Area and of the Province generally."

The Trust was established by a New Democratic government, but the previous Social Credit administration under Premier W.A.C. Bennett, who at times seemed bent on blacktopping the entire province, had made a specific exception for the Gulf Islands. They should be preserved just as they were, he declared. It was only coincidence, of course, that Bennett had recently bought a summer place on Salt Spring.

Bennett's conversion reflected the theme of "The Gulf Islanders Prayer":

"O Lord we thank Thee that by thy grace
Thou has brought us to this lovely place;
But now, O Lord, we humbly pray:
Thou shalt all others keep away"

Current disputes over preservation versus development have long been foretold. The Vancouver *Province* of June 5, 1927 (price five cents), ran a feature on the islands under the heading: "These Gulf Islands of Ours: Playgrounds for the Vancouver of the Future." Mainlanders and Vancouver Islanders had been enjoying bucolic weekends and summer holidays on the Gulf Islands long before

The Union Steamships' Cowichan, *which brought people and freight to the Gulf Islands.* (COURTESY BC ARCHIVES)

1927, however. Friction between residents and weekenders has been a fact of life on the islands since before the turn of the century. The "invasion" of the islands by 1960s dropouts brought back memories of early-day rustling and wood-pile thievery, among other problems. Today many of those once-derided "hippies" have become solidly entrenched in island communities, doing their best to keep out any new invasion.

Only the pace of future development of the islands is uncertain—that it will increase is inevitable. Those who still remember the islands as they used to be are the lucky ones. Life is not the same there now, but then it isn't anywhere else either.

These concerns are not those of this book, however. The attempt here is to invoke a sense of what it was like for the islands' first settlers. Fortunately for the historian, there is a legacy of memories and writings, of stories told and retold, to draw upon. Busy as many were, scratching out a living, the pioneers seemed to sense they were privileged people, enjoying some of the most beautiful scenery and salubrious weather in the world. As the following vignettes of some of their lives will attest, the islanders squeezed a lot of satisfaction and pleasure from their good fortune. Most led long, healthy lives.

It is fashionable nowadays to begin histories such as this with a detailed account of the rumblings which created the geology and shapes of the landscape millions of years ago. Also mandatory, it seems, is an attempt to re-tell the story of the Indians. After all, as is invariably pointed out, they were here first.

Both subjects are worthy of separate, full-length treatment. As Olivia Fletcher demonstrated in her informative and poetic book *Hammerstone*, on the making of Hornby Island, paleontology can be a lively subject. The history of the Indians is best left to the sciences of archaeology and anthropology. The truth is, we know little for certain of their society in the centuries before the white men took over. The Indians regarded the islands as many of us do today—a nice place to spend the summer, fishing and gathering clams. There were only a few permanent Indian settlements and they were small. They did, however, regard the islands as *their* land and shores, and strongly resented the intruders.

So this is an account, a celebration if you will, of the settlement of the islands during the century between the 1850s and the 1950s. These are the stories of some remarkable people and their some-times heroic endeavours to establish a way of life that has not yet been totally erased. It is good to be reminded of this past, to give us guideposts to the future. We can't go back to those days, but it should be possible to retain some of their quality.

Peter Murray, Victoria.

Farming, Parties
and Long Lives

"Take a Native woman and settle down." That was the advice usually given to newcomers and old Hudson's Bay Company hands in the middle of the last century by Governor James Douglas. Cast adrift by the winding down of the H.B.C.'s operations on the west coast, and failing to find their fortunes in the Fraser River or Cariboo gold rushes, many men heeded his words.

They did not all take native wives, but a surprising number did form lifetime partnerships with Indians. "Native women were trained from birth to live in the wilderness, a factor that added stability to their relationships with white men, especially during the early stages of establishing a homestead." Most learned quickly to speak English and proved adaptive to the ways of the white society. Some were remarkable women, not as subservient as their white counterparts, secure in the knowledge they could return to their tribes in the event of mistreatment.[1]

When the men began looking for a place to put down roots, they found that Douglas, despite his professed desire for settlers, had put too high a price on land for their meagre assets. The most desirable farmland near the markets of Victoria or the mouth of the Fraser River had been snapped up by former H.B.C. officers and Colonial Office insiders, often for speculation.

Looking northward on Vancouver Island, to the Cowichan, Chemainus and Comox valleys, many would-be settlers in the late 1850s learned that pre-emption fees and land-improvement requirements were still beyond their means. Some then turned to the Gulf Islands, where the land was less arable and the cost and problems of marketing produce would be greater, but the immediate price of acquiring a homestead was less. The opportunity to live cheaply off an abundant supply of deer, game birds and seafood was inviting. Clams and oysters were there for the gathering. "When the tide goes out the table is set" became a favourite islands' saying.

There were other reasons why the Gulf Islands attracted settlers. Not least was their accessibility, which may surprise present-day residents who have been heard to curse their dependence on an inadequate ferry service. But at the time of the early settlement period in the 1860s, there were few roads in the colony and land transportation was difficult. The simplest way to move people, lumber, livestock and supplies was by boat. Once arrived, the relative ease of travel in small boats gave the islanders a mobility and sociability that inland pioneers did not enjoy.

The hardest job facing the new settler was clearing the land. The first requirement was a small plot for a cabin and vegetable garden, followed by fields for grain and hay. Most of the islands were heavily forested, especially the valleys and pockets of arable land suitable for raising crops.

Some of the smaller trees were used to build log cabins, but the bigger ones were simply burned. There was no thought of wasting a valuable resource. Commercial logging did not exist in the first few decades of settlement. Even by 1906, when sawmills had been in operation for some time, less than one percent of the vast stands of coastal timber had been logged. "It is small wonder everyone thought then that here, surely, was enough timber to last forever."[2]

When getting rid of the big trees, the settlers simply cut them down, bored holes in the trunks which they filled with pitch or hot coals, and set them afire. "With a series of holes along a tree every six or eight feet you could burn up a whole tree in a day or two." The branches were disposed of separately in a slash fire. Stumps were dynamited and burned.[3]

If there was no danger of flames spreading out of control, standing trees were sometimes set afire. On Saturna Island, children occasionally turned big, pitch-drenched trees into giant torches just for the thrill. For their parents, tree removal was simply back-breaking work. A few who arrived in the 1870s and '80s directly from England with money, hired Chinese or Japanese labourers to do the job.

Other pioneers chose the hillier, less-treed areas of the islands which were ideal for unfenced sheep. The mild winters made early lambing possible. Other than cougars and wolves, which were soon eradicated, there were few wild predators, although eagles occasionally made off with new-born lambs and piglets. Humans rustling sheep and cattle were a more serious hazard for many years.

Most farms had a team of working oxen for plowing and pulling loads. Slow but sure and very strong, they were superior to horses for heavy work. In the days before roads, the island trails were too rough for horses. Because of the uneven ground, oxen pulled sleds or "stone-boats" rather than carts. Some sleds were fashioned from the crook of a tree.

Many farmers kept Yorkshire pigs for home-cured ham and bacon, and the pigs performed the extra service of turning over the soil in their hunt for food, clearing out roots so that stumps could be more easily dynamited. As well as common vegetables and tree fruits, the early farmers planted corn, melons and wheat. Grains were cut by hand with scythes and threshed with flails on granary floors.

One of the most useful items for homesteaders was an emptied five-gallon tin which had held coal oil for lamps. They were used as buckets and containers for just about everything—hauling water, taking away ashes, storing a variety of items. Some ingenious cabin-builders put a stack of tins together to make a chimney.

There was little waste on an early farm. Flour sacks served many purposes, including underwear. Sheepskins were tanned and made into mats, bed coverings and chair seats. Fat was saved to make soap, while mutton tallow greased boats and machinery and was made into candles. Sheep's wool was carded, spun and woven into clothing. Shakes were cut from felled cedar trees for roofs, while small timber poles were crafted into furniture, rafts, canoes, dragsleds and boats.

As might be expected from their diverse backgrounds, the first settlers met with varied degrees of success. Some observers were not impressed by what they found. Dr. Robert Brown, member of a government-sponsored "Exploration Committee" in 1864, complained that on Salt Spring and Vancouver Island the only ambition of too many homesteaders was "a log shanty, a pig, a potato patch, Klootchman (Indian woman) and a clam bed." Most had come to the area "attracted by the gold-fever and got their eyes jaundiced by their Cariboo failures, prodigal sons who are just waiting to get reconciled to their families, or to go home having mistaken their voca-

Cutting oats on a Saturna Island farm, ca *1910.* (COURTESY BC ARCHIVES)

tion." With no trade and few skills, they were "totally unacquainted with farming." Brown did admit, however, that he found little grumbling among these happy misfits.[4]

The majority were satisfied with their pleasant lifestyle. Their needs were few and it was almost possible to live off the land and sea, except for a few staples such as sugar, flour, salt, tea and matches. Coffee was made from burnt wheat bread. Many grew their own tobacco. Wild berries were abundant, as were salmon, deer, grouse and shellfish. Some settlers bought fish from the Indians. Said Salt Spring pioneer Joseph Akerman: "Anyone with a family, coming from the old country, could not strike an easier place to live in." Wallace Baikie, the son of a Denman Island pioneer, wrote: "The islanders raised large families and lived plain lives."[5]

It was especially pleasant for the children, who enjoyed an uncommon amount of freedom compared to their urban cousins. Barefoot all summer, they were always close to their surroundings. This bond to the natural world remained with them for the rest of their lives. They were taught at a young age how to handle boats, and the boys were given guns. "We all learned to row by the time we were four years old," said Dora Payne of Saturna. Most could swim before they were eight and were allowed to play with rafts and old dugout canoes.[6]

After the first wave of settlement in the 1860s by failed miners, wandering bachelors and drifters seeking to put down roots, there came a new kind of adventurer—one with money. Much has been made in local histories of the islands of the gay, carefree lives of the pioneers, but it is not the complete story. Many of these memoirs have been written by the descendants of the islands' privileged class, members of the British gentry who wanted for one reason or another (often simply a sense of adventure) to make a new life for themselves in a faraway British outpost. The lifestyle of these well-to-do settlers was mimicked by those who could afford it. The result was an inevitable tension between "working class" settlers and their more comfortable neighbours.

For the few, life seemed an endless round of pheasant shoots, picnics, cricket, tennis, regattas, bridge and poker games, parties and dances that went on till dawn so visitors from neighbouring islands could row home safely. The privileged belles wore dresses their indulgent parents had ordered from London, while the young men had Harris tweeds. There were well-stocked libraries and magazines from home. Frequent visits were made to Victoria, where some of the men kept permanent rooms for overnight stays. Hired hands looked after the farm while they were away.

But for others, like Pender Island farmer Robert Roe, life was not so soft. "I could never get away from work," he recalled. "My gosh, you can't take on a place like this and go around to picnics. It was nothing but work. No tennis-playing or anything else. . . . If you read the *Gulf Islands Patchwork* you would think it was very nice: lots of picnics, lots of tennis-playing, but I don't know. We could never get off for anything like that. There was always too many stumps to get out."[7]

It would be a mistake, however, to leave the impression that the upper-class emigrants from England were mere playboys. Most worked hard between the games. They also co-operated with their less-favoured neighbours on large projects such as barn-raising and the corralling and shearing of sheep. Despite strong political differences, they rallied round when anyone was in trouble. The strong individualism on the islands has always been coupled with a sense of community.

Times were especially hard for the English during the years of the First World War when cheques failed to arrive and many were forced to live off the land. After the war they found that their income from abroad did not stretch as far as it once had, and it took hard work to make a farm profitable. This new situation led to the introduction of the Farmers' Institutes which flourished in England. These co-operative movements allowed members to buy such essentials as fertilizer, seed, explosives and lime in bulk at reduced prices. The settlers also often bartered their produce—a barrel of herring for a barrel of apples, and so on.

One issue that united them was education. Schooling for the children was always a concern, and parents lobbied Victoria persistently for funds. At first, many taught their children at home. Only the well-off could afford to hire tutors or send their sons and daughters away to private boarding schools.

Another persistent issue was mail service. Infrequent steamship deliveries cut the islanders off from the outside world more than they cared to be. They argued that the lack of mail was discouraging further settlement.

Many of these discussions took place on the wharf while residents waited for the steamers to arrive. The docks were the community meeting place: gossip was exchanged and neighbours squabbled. They argued over the location of schoolhouses and roads, and of course, politics. The smaller the community, the more vehement people became in political disputes.

The building of roads had been an integral part of island life from the beginning. Since many of the small farms did not produce revenue, the men were allowed to pay off their taxes with road work. Under the Road Act of 1862 all male residents over 18 were required to perform six days of labour annually improving the rough tracks between settlements. Farmers with a team of horses and a wagon were obliged to supply them for road work two days each year. Thus it was the farmers who built the first proper roads, helping them get their produce to the wharves and onto steamships.

Meanwhile, transportation was also being improved on Vancouver Island and the mainland, making it harder for the Gulf Islands to compete. Fruit farming was severely curtailed around the turn of the century when ranchers in the Okanagan began producing a cheaper, earlier product which could be delivered by rail to Vancouver.

As farming generally became less profitable—except for the dairymen who shipped to the Salt Spring Island Creamery, a major islands' business—new sources of income were sought. Logging operations expanded, particularly on the northern islands of Denman, Hornby and Lasqueti. The quarrying of shale and sandstone also prospered for a time.

Enterprising Japanese-Canadian settlers operated large tomato-growing hothouses on Mayne Island, as well as herring and salmon salteries on some of the other islands. The Japanese and Indians also harvested seaweed which they dried and ground up as a food additive. The Second World War, however, put an end to all the Japanese enterprises.

11

Smaller industries included the cutting of poles or "props" for the coal mines of Nanaimo and Cumberland. Some were shipped as far away as the silver mines of Mexico and South America. Many men left the islands in the summer months to fish commercially or take wage-earning jobs as loggers and cannery workers to tide their families over the winter.

Some events were common to all or most of the islands. On a Sunday in June 1886, a great cloud of smoke drifted from the east across the Strait of Georgia. Only later did island residents learn of the fire that levelled the early town of Vancouver. A drought in 1895 dried up many island wells, a phenomenon persisting today and obviously caused not just by increased population. Wallace Baikie remembered watching Halley's Comet in 1910 for several days in a row as it passed through the night sky. Huge forest fires often raged unchecked for weeks, and many summers were marred by a pall of smoke hanging over the strait.

For Mrs. Stanley Page of Galiano a vivid memory was the smell of dead salmon in the summertime. "These were deposited on the beaches by the hundreds. There were heads, tails, whole fish and parts of fish all brought to us by the ebb tide from the Fraser River in the fishing season."[8]

On Sunday morning, June 23, 1946, an earthquake centred in the Campbell River area was felt throughout the islands, most strongly on Hornby and Denman, where subsurface waterways were altered and a number of wells went dry.

The winter of 1916 is recalled as the year of the big snowfall—up to six feet covering roadways on some islands, blocking travel for weeks. That was the most severe on record, but there have been many other hard winters and harsh storms, giving the lie to many magazine stories comparing the islands' climate to that of California. Pleasant and relatively mild it is compared to the rest of Canada, but tropical it is not.

A lot of nonsense has been written about the islands over the years—much of it aimed at selling real estate—but none more than about climate. One B.C. writer who should have known better wrote that the Japanese Current kept the Gulf Islands warm all the year round. The current does more for Tofino and the Queen Charlotte Islands than it does for the Strait of Georgia. The Fraser River has more effect on the strait's temperature: warmer fresh water rises to the top and raises the mercury with it.

One of the most intriguing discoveries that a researcher makes delving into the lives of the Gulf Islanders is the unusual longevity of the early settlers. The number of men and women who lived into their 80s and 90s, and even past the century mark, is astonishing. It is all the more remarkable when it is remembered that this was before modern wonder drugs and medical technology.

The easy explanation for this phenomenon is that the people lived idyllic, healthy, stress-free lives isolated from the epidemics and diseases of the cities. Their diets were rich and varied. They had almost continual outdoor exercise, working the fields, rowing their boats and playing sports for recreation. These conditions no doubt contributed to the long lives recorded on the islands, but they were not unique and there must be other reasons.

One theory holds that because the islanders' activities were so linked to the tides, they took on some of the ageless rhythm of the ocean in their minds and bodies. That may be a poetic answer, but it is not one that lends itself to measurement or analysis. It does tie in, however, to the common background of many settlers—they, or their parents, came to the Gulf Islands from other islands.

The number of families from the Shetland and Orkney Islands of Scotland is striking: the Mouats of Salt Spring, the Georgesons of Galiano and Mayne, and the Baikies and McFarlans of Denman are only a few of the best known. Hawaiians also made up a sizable proportion of the early Salt Spring Island population and inter-married with the other races.

It appears that the answer to Gulf Islands longevity may lie in genetics as much as any other factor. Or it could be that the contented islanders were simply unwilling to end a good thing.

13

A Kidnapping, Saloons and Tomatoes

For multitudes of tourists, Active Pass is the highlight of their non-stop ferry voyage between the mainland and Vancouver Island. The imposing bluffs of Galiano on the north side of the narrow passage, the treed shores of Mayne on the south which have changed little in the past century, the jade-green water surging in swift tidal currents with gulls and eagles overhead—all are magnets for the ubiquitous camera. In earlier days, the pass was noted more for being a stop-over point, a sheltered spot to rest and restock before venturing into the open water of the Strait of Georgia.

Bound for the Fraser River sandbars, thousands of gold-hunters travelled through in 1858 from Victoria, some in large passenger steamboats but many in a ragged fleet of canoes, rowboats and little sailing craft, pausing at Miners Bay on Mayne in a corner of the pass.

At first the bay was simply a camping spot, a meadow behind a sloping beach with two freshwater streams nearby. Gradually, a little community grew up to serve the needs of the travellers, and the first permanent settlers followed soon after. With a broad, arable valley running eastward across the island from Miners Bay, Mayne was an enticing spot for prospective farmers. The gently rolling land lent itself to intensive agriculture more than any of the other islands.

The first land pre-emptions, of 100 acres each, were taken out in 1861 by Christian Mayers and James Greavy. The two men teamed up to buy a small sloop to carry their produce to markets in Victoria and New Westminster, but neither settled permanently on the island. Greavy left after repeated losses of cattle and hogs to rustlers, who butchered the animals and sold the meat in Nanaimo. In 1867 a resident of the pass area identified as James Stephens was charged after attempting to enlist one of Greavy's hired hands in the thievery.

Like the first settlers on Salt Spring, whose pre-emptions preceded those on Mayne by a couple of years, the early Mayne Islanders were plagued by Indian violence. The perpetrators were mostly from the war-like Lamalchi band of Cowichan Indians on Kuper Island. There were only a dozen or so Cowichans who resided permanently on Mayne, at Helen Point near the western entrance to Active Pass, and they caused no problems for the newcomers.

The first and most dramatic incident of Indian violence occurred in April of 1863, after Mayers had invited his friend Frederick Marks to move with his family from Waldron Island in the San Juans. The family was sailing up Plumper Sound in two vessels when they were separated by a sudden squall. Mrs. Marks, their four small children and the unidentified skipper of their craft managed to ride out the storm and reach Miners Bay. Marks and his young married daughter, Caroline Harvey, 15, were in the second boat, which was forced to take shelter on the south shore of Saturna near Croker Point, subsequently known as Murder Point. They were making camp on the beach when they were attacked and slain by a Lamalchi band. Their bodies were believed to have been weighted with stones and thrown into deep water; they were never recovered. Mayers and other searchers found only their smashed boat, the remains of a campfire, and the Marks's two dogs, alive and well.

The Royal Navy went into action immediately. Lieutenant-Commander H.D. Lascelles of H.M.S *Forward* was ordered by Douglas to avoid taking Indian lives in the hunt for the murderers, but action against their property was approved. The area was searched for six weeks, during which time a number of Indian villages were blasted by cannon balls, before 14 men and four women Lamalchis were captured at Collinson Point on Galiano Island. They were charged in the murder of Marks and his daughter, as well as the death of a seaman killed aboard the *Forward* by gunfire from shore while the Kuper Island village was being bombarded. Four men were hanged on July 4, 1863, in front of the Victoria police barracks. Douglas subsequently appointed Major John Peter Mouat Biggs, who had served 25 years in India, as justice of the peace for the islands, based in Chemainus.

After Mayers and Greavy, one of the earliest settlers was Nicholas Cook, who took up 100 acres in 1864. Cook had earlier taken part in the Fraser River gold rush and while there had married a handsome Lillooet Indian woman, Catherine "Kitty". The Cooks had three boys. One of them, John, was born in 1865. When he was about three years old he apparently wandered away to the beach where he was kidnapped by a group of Haidas canoeing through the pass. They were returning to the Queen Charlotte Islands from Victoria, and the boy was kept as a slave for the next ten years. Then in 1878, when the Haidas took him south on one of their annual trading junkets, young Cook recognized his former home site as the canoes threaded their way through the pass and managed to escape. He found his mother but was dismayed to learn that since his father had died at 38 in 1870, she had married another pioneer, Jacob Heck.

Details of this remarkable story are sketchy and nothing is known of the time John Cook spent with the Haidas. In later life he spoke to few about his adventure and the only account comes from a neighbour on Galiano Island, Mary Backlund.

After a brief reunion with his mother, young John left home and went to work on Governor Douglas's farm on the Saanich Peninsula. "Then he ran away again," Mrs. Backlund recounted. "He seemed to always be running away, somehow or another." When he was about 17 John came under the wing of pioneer Henry "Scotty" Georgeson, Mrs. Backlund's great grandfather, who persuaded him to take up land on the east side of Galiano. He married, had three children, and grew apples on his 160-acre property for 66 years at what is now known as Cook's Bay. A big, powerful man, Cook also worked as a labourer on other Galiano farms, and was noted for his ability to build fine split-rail fences. John Cook died in 1955 at the age of 89. Mrs. Backlund said Cook became deaf in his later years and spoke little, and few people knew of his early life. He apparently confided in Mary Backlund because of her relationship with his mentor and the fact that he was fond of his neighbours. "We were close friends," she said. "He took quite a liking to us."[1]

In 1870 there had been another violent incident on Mayne, which resulted in the hanging of an Indian convicted of murder. Robert Clarke had been a tinker in Victoria before moving with his native wife Annie and three children to the Village Bay area. While Annie was visiting on Galiano, Clarke was found shot to death outside his cabin, which had been looted. A $500 reward was posted by police for the murderer and an Indian known only as "Tom" was captured and hanged in 1873.[2]

Despite these incidents, new settlers continued to arrive on the island, many of them gold hunters who had given up on the Cariboo rush which followed the Fraser stampede. Jacob Heck and John Puetz had been partners for a time in the Cariboo and in 1870 they pre-empted 120 acres each in the valley behind Miners Bay.

Another former miner was W.T. "Tom" Collinson, who pre-empted 160 acres near the south end of the island. Long and lean, the bearded Collinson loved to tell tall tales and became known as "the Baron Munchausen of Mayne." He opened a store in his home at Miners Bay and became the island's first postmaster in 1880. Until the government built a wharf in 1878, the settlers rowed out into the pass to intercept the steamers and give letters to the purser for posting. When Collinson took over, a slot was cut in the wall of his house for mailing letters. On mail days Collinson opened the bags on his verandah and handed mail to residents gathered around. Galiano and Pender islanders also rowed over for their mail.

In 1895 Tom and his Indian wife Mary turned their home into a boarding-house. The Collinsons had three daughters: Emma, Elizabeth and Margaret, and three sons: Melville, Samuel and James. Melville and Sam both shipped out on schooners based in Victoria to hunt fur seals in the North Pacific, along with Mayne Islanders Hunter Jack and Joseph Bodine.

Other early settlers included John Silva, a young Portuguese seaman who had jumped ship in Victoria in 1852. He earned enough money to run a grocery store there for a time, before moving in 1873 with his Indian wife Louisa and their family to 237 acres on Village Bay. After two of their ten children drowned in the pass, a despondent Louisa wanted to leave. Joe was discouraged over the persistent rustling of their sheep, so the Silvas sold out to the Deacon family in 1883 and moved to Gabriola Island.[3]

John Deacon was born in Ontario and his wife Margaret was Irish. John arrived on Mayne in 1879; his family followed in 1883. Besides operating their 300-acre "Hardscrabble Farm," the Deacons ran a boarding-house at Village Bay. Their son Dalton later took over the operation and lived for 77 years on the island. During times when farming was uneconomic he turned the pasture into a rudimentary public golf course and catered to the golfers. John Deacon died in hospital at Ganges in 1922, aged 93.

Fred Robson had left England in 1862 at 14 aboard the "bride ship" *Robert Lowe* to join his father, an artist with Canadian Pacific Railway survey parties in the B.C. interior. The youth tried prospecting in the Cariboo, and made a brief attempt at homesteading in the Fraser Valley. With his last two dollars he bought a leaky dugout canoe which he patched with tin and paddled from the mainland to Horton Bay on Mayne in 1871. John Ackholm helped him build a log house and clear a patch of land. Robson went into partnership with Tom Collinson for a time, before being joined by his brother William and his family. They established "Glenwood Farm," noted for its prize Jersey cattle. Robson took his produce to Victoria by canoe and paid his taxes each year by selling his fattest cow to a butcher in the capital.

In the early days, big sailing vessels had shunned Active Pass because of the narrow, twisting channel and its tidal currents. Now, with the steady increase of steamship traffic, it was decided that a lighthouse was needed to mark the eastern entrance at Georgina Point on Mayne. The light was completed in 1885 and the first keeper appointed by the federal government was Henry Georgeson, a Shetland Islands native.

"Scotty" Georgeson had run away from home in 1849 at the age of 14 after being beaten by a school teacher. It was also a time of famine in the Shetlands and Georgeson was one of 15 children at the family table, five of whom settled in B.C. He was another ship-jumper at Victoria who joined the Fraser River gold rush. Georgeson lived with Sophie, a Lillooet native woman, and ran a hotel near Yale before settling on Galiano Island. He served for a time as assistant keeper on the Sandheads Light Ship at the mouth of the Fraser before moving to the new light on Mayne. He was required to marry Sophie formally to qualify for the lighthouse positions.

In 1893, after a new, steam-powered foghorn had been installed, the first on the coast, Georgeson succeeded in getting his son George appointed as assistant. Scotty was regarded as a wizard with a steam engine, but occasionally the machinery failed and he or his son was forced to ring the bell by hand when steamers blew their whistles approaching the pass in fog. The lights in those days were coal-oil lamps with wicks and chimneys, with a revolving, many-faceted magnifying glass. The glass was wound up every six or seven hours and kept going with a system of chains and weights.

The foghorn was functioning normally at about one P.M. on October 13, 1918, when the station's only major mishap occurred. The *Princess Adelaide* failed to sound her whistle until she was almost upon the rocks. When Scotty's grandson Archie peered out into the mist, there was the looming hull of the big passenger steamer, as he put it, "stuck right in front of the lighthouse like a great big city."[4]

The steamer's propeller was sheered off, her rudder knocked askew and she was hung up on the rocks only a hundred yards in front of the light for three days before tugs pulled her free. The Georgesons spent the first day towing passengers ashore in lifeboats. They were cared for by island residents until the *Princess Alice* arrived to take them on to Victoria.

Henry "Scotty" Georgeson, wearing his long-service medal for his years at Georgina Point lighthouse. (COURTESY BC ARCHIVES)

Georgeson stayed on at Georgina Point for 35 years until his retirement in 1921, when he was succeeded by his son George. Grandsons Archie and Jack, George's sons, built a replica of the Active Pass Light on his Galiano property where he lived with another son and grandchildren until his death in 1927 at 93. For five decades, members of the Georgeson family were in the lighthouse service, at Active Pass, East Point on Saturna, Portlock Point on Prevost Island, and Albert Head south of Victoria. Scotty's brothers Arthur and Edward both became ship pilots on the coast.

On December 4, 1885, a new, larger wharf had been completed at Miners Bay, replacing the one built only seven years before. The first steamer to dock was the *Princess Louise*, on her way from New Westminster to Victoria. Bunting strung on the wharf flapped in the breeze and settlers saluted the steamer's arrival by firing rifles. To mark the occasion, orchardist Thomas Figg presented an illuminated scroll to Premier William Smithe aboard the *Louise*. Smithe had begun his political career as M.L.A. for Cowichan and the Islands and during his four years as premier, between 1883 and 1887, his constituents were the recipients of a number of public works improvements.

After the shipboard ceremony the premier and other dignitaries went ashore to John Puetz's new hotel and store for refreshments. Puetz was active in Mayne affairs and had been rewarded by the government with appointments as justice of the peace, assessor and tax collector. There was little work involved in any of the positions since the population of the island didn't reach a hundred until the turn of the century.

After the few early incidents of violence, crime was mostly against property—theft of boats, cattle rustling, and smuggling. Most occurred during the summer months when traffic was heavy through the pass to and from the Fraser River canneries. When appeals by the settlers could no longer be ignored, the provincial police appointed Arthur Drummond of Saturna Island in 1894 as patrol officer for the Gulf Islands, based on Mayne. A jailhouse measuring only 15 by 23 feet, with a small room for the magistrate and two cells, was built at Miners Bay in 1896 on property sold to the government by Warburton Pike. It still stands today, as a museum. Until the jail was completed and a stove and table provided for him, Drummond boarded at Robson's hotel. Drummond was a scion of Drummond Castle in Scotland, with two brothers, Bertie "Red Drummond" and Walter "Old Black". A talented violinist, Walter had a little store and post office at the Saturna wharf; sometimes he would deliver orders by boat.

The first clergyman to visit Mayne on a regular basis was Canon Arthur J. Beanlands of Victoria, who preached one Sunday a month, from 1889 to 1891, at the Miners Bay schoolhouse, which had been opened in 1885 with 20 pupils. Bishop William W. Perrin ministered to the islanders for three years after 1893, sometimes rowing from Sidney. Then, in 1896, Canon William Francis Locke Paddon took over the ministry.

Paddon had travelled to B.C. from Ireland in 1885, seeking a more healthful environment. He liked what he found and returned for his family, emigrating in 1889 with his wife, seven sons, two daughters and tutor Alfred Cook. Canon Paddon served the Anglican Church in Victoria for a number of years before his Mayne posting. He continued to live in Victoria until 1904, commuting to the island twice a month on the steamer.

Paddon's first task was to get a church built. Warburton Pike, an entrepreneur and adventurer living on Saturna, donated four acres on a hill overlooking the pass. The property included a house built by Thomas Figg about 1889 which was used for services and meetings, after an inside wall was knocked down, until the church was built. A fund established for the purchase of a steam launch for a Gulf Islands Mission was allotted by Bishop Perrin for the construction of the church. The contractor was William Cain of Galiano and the Church of St. Mary Magdalene was consecrated by the bishop on Easter Sunday, April 17, 1898. The steeple became a landmark for ships in the pass.

Two years later the church acquired a unique baptismal font. While prowling the shoreline on Saturna near East Point, lightkeeper James Georgeson, Scotty's brother, discovered an unusually shaped sandstone block with a wave-carved basin. Georgeson mentioned his find to Ralph Grey of nearby Samuel Island, who had been appointed to the church board along with representatives from a number of other islands. (Grey used to take a load of butter from his farm to sell on Mayne when he rowed over for meetings.) The stone weighed 400 pounds, but Grey, Georgeson, Evan Hooson of Pender and Paddon succeeded in hoisting it into a rowboat. Paddon and Grey rowed with the stone to Bennett Bay from where it was transported by cart to be installed in the church, where it still stands.

In 1904 the old Figg house adjacent to the church was renovated and enlarged, and the Paddon family moved over from Victoria. This first vicarage burned down March 17, 1907, with only some furniture and books rescued. A bucket brigade of residents saved the church. The Paddons lived in two tents until a new residence was completed.

Paddon was a fire-and-brimstone preacher who wore his black surplice most of the time and was a strict disciplinarian with his family. Stubborn and durable, he kept a stable lantern in the bottom of his rowboat which he placed under a cape over his knees to keep his feet and legs warm on winter visits to parishioners. In 1896 Paddon had been a passenger on the streetcar which plunged into Victoria's Gorge waterway when the old Point Ellice bridge collapsed. Fifty-five people perished in the mishap, but Paddon escaped with nervous shock and bruises. He had been pulled unconscious from the water and resuscitated on the nearby lawn of Captain William Grant. He told his rescuers later that the experience of being revived was much worse than the sensation of drowning.

Canon Paddon retired in March 1922, and died at 78 that August in the hospital at Ganges. He had left instructions that the burial service be held at five A.M., "since he knew only the parishioners who loved him would rise that early to attend his funeral."[5]

If Mayne was the hub of the southern Gulf Islands, then the famed old Point Comfort Hotel was for a long time the centre of their social life. It was also the forerunner of Gulf Island hostelries catering to summer visitors from the mainland. It was an ambitious undertaking for its time—a three-storey, 35-room mansion with a grand spiral staircase, large dining-room, elegant furnishings and an inviting bar. The setting was unmatched: 138 choice acres close by the lighthouse with spectacular views of the Strait of Georgia, the mainland mountains and ships entering Active Pass.

The hotel was financed by a number of investors, including steamship company owner Captain John Irving, Weiler Brothers Furniture Company of Victoria, and Mayne resident W.H. Mawdsley, on whose property it was built. Warburton Pike held a mortgage on the building and was listed in the prospectus as "proprietor." The hotel opened for business in 1893. The first guests, mostly successful gold miners able to winter in a mild climate, were drawn to the bar and spent their hard-earned cash there. Much of the food came from Mawdsley's previously developed farm on the property.

So "Little Hell," as Mayne with its saloons was called on the other, more temperate, islands, lived up to its name, at least in the dark months. The summers were mostly quiet except for a few day-trippers or weekenders who arrived by ferry or chartered vessel. In 1895, after Mawdsley got into financial difficulties, Pike foreclosed on a $2,500 mortgage and placed pioneers Thomas and Alice Bennett in charge of running the hotel.

Despite competition from the boarding-houses operated by such pioneer families as the Deacons, Collinsons and Robsons (the only one with a saloon), the Point Comfort Hotel carried on until its sale in 1900. After leaving the hotel, the Bennetts moved to the southeast end of the island, where Bennett Bay was named after them. Mrs. Bennett was a midwife for Mayne and the adjacent islands.

The new owner was Eustace Downman Maude, an imposing 6'6" retired Royal Navy commander, and his wife Grace. They paid $2,500 for the hotel and property, which now included a tennis court and cricket pitch. The Maudes intended to continue running it as a hotel, but gave up the business after three years and turned it into their private residence. A militant teetotaller, Grace Maude had begun by closing down the bar, which cost the hotel much of its revenue and clientele. Uneasy with the Chinese help hired to serve summer visitors, she gave up the hotel business with a sense of relief.[6]

For the next 20 years the Maudes and their four children lived on in the mansion, continuing to give elegant parties while the building gradually disintegrated around them. For lack of interest, or funds, they neglected maintenance. Shingles blown off the roof on blustery winter days were not replaced. When water collapsed the plaster in an upstairs bedroom, the Maudes simply moved to another one.

The Maudes maintained a stately aplomb in the face of such minor inconveniences. During one memorable dinner party Reverend Hubert Payne of Saturna Island was sitting next to Mrs. Maude "when a huge piece of plaster fell from the ceiling, missing the Rev. Payne's head by inches. In a very short time the dining room floor was covered with water. Commander Maude's son, George, arrived quickly on the scene with an auger drilling tool. Soon he had drilled a number of holes in the floor so the water could escape."

When Mrs. Maude was cleaning up after one of the parties or dances in the rainy season she often had to put on gumboots. In the winter the Maudes moved to bedrooms at the back of the house, sheltered from the cold northeast winds.

Eventually, "when the foundations of the house started to give way and doors refused to close," the Maudes decided to sell. Point Comfort was no longer comfortable. They moved into "Comfort Cottage" on an adjacent property. During the First World War Mrs. Maude taught the Mayne Island girls how to knit.[7]

Eustace Maude was obviously chafing at his quiet landlubber life after so many years at sea. He flitted around the island in his 22-foot *Half-Moon*, a sailing yawl with an auxiliary gas engine, but that didn't satisfy his wanderlust, so at the age of 77 in 1925 he set out alone, bound for Panama and then on to England. His concerned son tried to dissuade him, but Maude replied simply, "Why not?"

Maude took along a one-volume edition of Shakespeare's plays, Captain J.C. Voss's account of his round-the-world voyage in *Tilikum*, and other favourite books. He didn't have much chance to get into his reading material, however. Three weeks after leaving Victoria he ran into a violent storm off Eureka, California, on May 20. A boom hit him in the back of his head, knocking him unconscious. He suffered violent pain for many days, from an apparent concussion, and was almost blinded by the headache and unremitting sun. He was sighted by a freighter on June 18 some 600 miles off the coast but stubbornly declined assistance. Unable to read his compass, Maude somehow managed to get back to Cape Flattery on his own and was towed into Neah Bay on August 9 after being blown about for five days. In 97 days he had travelled 4,000 miles. Maude's son went over to bring the aging adventurer home. Maude died on Mayne in 1929, aged 81; his wife Grace was 85 when she died in 1946.[8]

The new owners of the big house were Colonel and Lady Constance Fawkes, who had sold their aged mansion in Bedhampton, England. They stayed with the Maudes for a time before deciding to buy the property in 1924. Lady Constance was the daughter of the Marquis of Ailsa in Scotland; her husband, Lionel Grimston Fawkes, was an ex-army officer and accomplished artist.

Jack Borradaile of Salt Spring Island, who served the Fawkes for 20 years as their man Friday, recalled the stir caused among the islanders the day the couple arrived on the *Otter* at Miners Bay: "Colonel Fawkes was wearing a black suit and straw hat (his suit was more gray than black, I am sure it had not been cleaned for months), over his right shoulder hung his leather water bottle and over his left shoulder was his canvas bag which contained sketching pads and paints. He carried his easel in his hand. Lady Constance was wearing a black gown with a full length coat, the hem of which had been

Lady Constance Fawkes. (COURTESY BC ARCHIVES)

thoroughly chewed by her pet dog in England. On her feet she had high gumboots." She may have been a titled Lady, but Constance had no vanity. Her clothes and hairdo were plain, and she padded down the 90-foot hallways in tennis shoes.[9]

Carpenters, plumbers and electricians were immediately put to work restoring the building to a semblance of its former grandeur. Running water and electric light were installed and the mansion was named "Culzean," (pronounced "Ku-Lane") after Culzean Castle in Ayrshire where Lady Constance had spent her childhood.[10]

Settled into their new home, the colonel and his lady began each day with a cold bath. Sometimes in the winter when the pipes were frozen Borradaile would break the ice on the rain-water tank and carry buckets of water to the upstairs bathrooms. During the day Lady Constance cooked, worked on her loom or sewed underwear for needy children in the East End of Vancouver. The housekeeper, a Mrs. Hogben, cleaned up after her. Rain or shine, the colonel set off with his sketch pad to various vantage points in the vicinity.

Thursday afternoons were set aside for tennis in summer and for parlour games in the dining-room in winter. After the games tea was served, under a cherry tree beside the house when the weather permitted. At Christmas, the Fawkes invited up to 40 guests for dinner. The house and grounds were often made available for charitable events, which included croquet and clock golf on the lawn.

Lady Constance was also instrumental in organizing the island's first fall fair in the summer of 1925 at the Miners Bay Community Hall, which is still standing as the Mayne Island Agricultural Society Hall. The society took it over in 1963. The hall had been built about 1900 and was the site of the island's annual New Year's Eve dance, followed by a New Year's Day party. The other big celebration on Mayne was May 24, when residents from neighbouring islands came over for the picnic, footraces and dance at the community hall.

The Fawkes were both devout Anglicans. Lionel read from the Bible after breakfast and prayed, and was a founder of the island's Sunday school. Lady Constance was of an evangelistic persuasion and with a small group of friends went to the wharf on boat-days with a portable organ to sing hymns. Jack Borradaile joined in by reading aloud from the Scriptures. Their little performance added to the carnival spirit of boat-day excursions.[11]

Colonel Lionel Fawkes. (COURTESY BC ARCHIVES)

Colonel Fawkes died at Culzean in 1931, aged 82, and was buried in the little cemetery overlooking Active Pass. His estate included two original works by the great English landscape artist, J.M.W. Turner, to go to his nieces in England after his wife's death. Fawkes's grandfather had been a patron of Turner and the family's ancestral home in Yorkshire at one time had the largest collection in the world. During the last ten years of Lady Constance's life these two paintings were on loan to the Vancouver Art Gallery. Borradaile describes taking them on the *Princess Mary* to Vancouver, wrapped in brown paper, and carrying them under his arm from the wharf to the gallery.

Lady Constance and Borradaile left Culzean in the hands of caretakers in 1942 and moved to Vancouver for two years. After their return Borradaile, who at 40 appeared headed for a life of bachelorhood, married in 1945 a young housekeeper who had been a short time at the mansion. A year later Lady Constance died at the age of 91, leaving her entire estate to Borradaile. It included such valuables as George the Third silverware, Dresden china and French furniture that had never been unpacked, but after estate taxes of $45,000 were paid there was little left from the proceeds. Culzean, one of the Gulf Islands' best-known landmarks, was sold in 1946 for $13,500 and torn down 12 years later.

Before going to work for the Fawkes at the age of 19, Borradaile had lived with his family on Salt Spring Island. His mother was one of the five daughters of Reverend Edward F. Wilson. Like Grace Maude, Borradaile was a foe of the demon rum: "The large room that was once the Bar was still intact when I first went to Culzean in 1925. I had the pleasure of wrecking it and making a very charming room for myself."[12]

Borradaile stayed on at Culzean with his wife and a handyman for nine months, then moved to Victoria with ten tons of furniture and numerous packing cases. Included in the estate were 400 paintings by Colonel Fawkes, some of which were donated to the Provincial Archives.

The settlement of Mayne continued in the early years of the new century. One of the noteworthy arrivals was Scottish-born John Aitken. He came to B.C. in 1881, working as a logger, beachcomber, prospector and farmhand for Horatio Robertson for two years on Moresby Island and later on Max Enke's Galiano Island farm. His brother Alex worked for a time as a shepherd on the big Musgrave sheep ranch on Salt Spring.

John Aitken landed on Mayne in 1908, buying a home and store at Miners Bay. In 1920 Aitken bought the Paddons' Horton Bay farm, where he ran sheep and cut and sold firewood. A quiet man, he was a good shot and an expert cougar hunter. Aitken also grew prize flowers. After his retirement in 1946 the farm was taken over by his son Roy, who had worked with his father for years. The Aitkens had a famed ox named "William" which stayed in harness for 36 years, pulling a plow and hauling wood in a two-wheeled cart.

Richard Hall, a member of a wealthy English family in Cheshire, had studied to be an agriculturalist on Guernsey in the Channel Islands. Moving to Canada, he first tried his luck at farming in Saskatchewan. Unhappy on the prairies, he came to fairer climes in the Gulf Islands. His first stop was Thetis Island, where he worked as a farmhand for a time, and then he bought James Island, off the Saanich Peninsula, with his brothers Charles and Reginald. Eventually, in 1910, Hall landed on Mayne, where he bought some land from the Maudes' old Point Comfort Hotel property.

It was here that Hall built the island's first greenhouses for tomato-growing, before enlisting in 1914. He hired two Chinese gardeners who lived in a cottage on the property. After returning from the war Hall moved to the valley behind Miners Bay, where he expanded his hothouse operation. Employing Japanese labourers, Hall grew daffodils and tomatoes in greenhouses so large that horses pulled plows inside. A small sawmill was built on the island to supply boards for the tomato crates, which were shipped by steamer to Vancouver. Because of the sunnier climate, the Gulf Island tomatoes were at least two weeks ahead of the Fraser delta product. Encouraged by Hall's success, James Bennett and Hunter Jack of Mayne also went into the business.

An attempt was made to start a brickyard at Bennett Bay but the project was aborted when the investors ran out of money. The only reminder was a boarding-house built for the workers which remained empty until 1942. It then became the Arbutus Lodge for a time and later the Mayne Inn.

It was tourism, the island's first industry, which continued to flourish. Some of the small hostelries established in the 1800s were enlarged and new ones were established. Tom Collinson's daughter Emma and her husband Brook Naylor took over Tom's old boarding-house after he died in 1911 and renamed it Grandview Lodge. They lured fishermen to the lodge with the promise of fresh salmon from Active Pass. Emma was recognized as one of the top rowboat guides in the area.

"Mrs. Naylor was the lady bountiful of the Island," Jack Borradaile wrote. "If anyone was sick, she would pack a basket with some of her delicious home-made bread, cake and cookies and a jar of soup which only Mrs. Naylor could make. She was known for her wonderful cooking. To her hotel guests it was one of the main attractions." The Grandview Lodge later became Springwater Lodge, today the province's oldest continually operating inn.

The old Point Comfort Hotel reopened for a time as the Cherry Tree Inn after the Second World War, but failed once again. Richard Hall and his wife, the former Nesta Steward of Galiano, turned their large home above Miners Bay into a guest house, "The Anchorage."[13]

Bert Emery, a druggist by training, operated a successful general store at the Miners Bay wharf during the 1920s. Built by Tom Collinson, the store had a number of owners over the years. Emery later moved to Vancouver, where he became active in civic politics.

In the 1930s Richard and Eva Steele, who had been tending sheep for a rancher on Saturna, looked for a way to make enough money to acquire property of their own. Eva was an expert cook who had brought a special plum-pudding recipe with her from England. After some experimentation, the Steeles started canning the pudding. On making their first big sale to a Vancouver department store, the Steeles moved their small canning operation to Mayne, where they acquired part of Hunter Jack's Springhill Farm property, including the farm buildings. They used the name "Springhill Cannery" on their labels.

The business prospered until the war, when there was a shortage of tin. The plum puddings were ruled to be a luxury item, so the Steeles switched to stews, for which they were allotted 100 tins per week to be shipped to isolated northern B.C. communities. It was sold as "Steele's All Beef Stew." Pudding production resumed after the war with eight employees but poor health forced the Steeles to sell out to a mainland firm in 1949. The cannery remained on the island until 1953 when ferry service cutbacks forced the company to move to Vancouver.[14]

Most of the Gulf Islands had residents of Japanese origin, but Mayne had the largest community. By 1938 they made up a third of the island's population of 186, and produced half of its crops. The influx had begun in the 1890s when Japanese workmen were ferried across the Strait of Georgia after the fishing season ended in the fall to cut cordwood for the steam furnaces of the Fraser River canneries. The wood was shipped back on a variety of small boats, including skiffs, sloops and schooners. The Japanese also dug pits to make charcoal for heating soldering irons in the canneries, and made floats for fishnets.

Japanese fishermen operating out of Horton Bay were offered work by settlers in the off-season clearing land and working on farms. Before long a few had saved enough to rent or buy land and settle. Some were employed by Richard Hall in his greenhouses, others began raising chickens. Another source of income for the Japanese was exporting dried seaweed.

It was not long before the Japanese had learned enough about the greenhouse business to go into it on their own. Raising poultry had proved uneconomic, so they formed a tomato-growing association in the 1930s that produced 50 tons a year.[15]

The Japanese also tried dairy farming, but with less success. Their butter, which they sold to John Aitken's store, went rancid after two days and there were few buyers. Not wanting to hurt their feelings, Aitken dumped the butter off the end of the wharf at night. "He lost out on the butter, but he kept their trade," said Mrs. Peter Georgeson, Aitken's daughter. Once when butter was piled up at the store and there was no time to throw it off the wharf, Aitken mixed it with seal oil to smear on skid-road logs.[16]

Then the war changed everything on the island. It was close to midnight on December 7, 1941, and Zeiji Teramoto had just finished checking his tomato hothouse when the Royal Canadian Mounted Police arrived and led him away. His wife and seven frightened children were left behind. Three other Mayne Island Japanese farmers were also arrested that night and taken off the island. In 1942 the remaining Japanese were uprooted from their homes and properties and sent away from the coast to internment camps for the duration of the war, a sad chapter in the history of the Gulf Islands and the rest of British Columbia. On Mayne, the departure of so many children forced the closure of the school for two years.

On April 21, 1942, when the 50 remaining Japanese men, women and children left on the *Princess Mary*, many islanders came to the dock for tearful farewells. A number of residents hid precious belongings of their former neighbours, to be returned after the war ended. Some tried to buy Japanese land and hold it for them, but in 1944 the federal government made that a criminal offence. Legislation had been passed two years previously, enabling returning servicemen to buy the confiscated lands. A few residents managed to keep the Japanese-built greenhouses operating during the war by renting them from a government agency, but they were taken over after 1945. Japanese fishboats, seized by the navy after the attack on Pearl Harbor, were towed to the Fraser River and sold off in 1942.

Immigrant pioneers from the British Isles were not as dominant on Mayne as they were on neighbouring islands. The Japanese played a larger role there than on any of the other Gulf Islands, mixing easily into the island's diverse racial make-up. A number of the early settlers were of German descent and there were many mixed marriages with Indian women. It was this cosmopolitan population, combined with Mayne's geographic position, that made it the social centre of the outer Gulf Islands for many years.

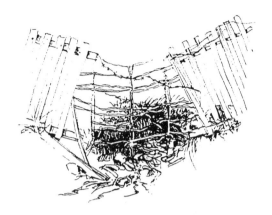

Musical Bachelors and a Cowbell

Settlement on Galiano proceeded more slowly than on Mayne. Although much larger, Galiano had less arable land, and most of the island was thickly forested with fir and cedar. Ranchers occupied isolated pockets along the eastern and western shores of the long, narrow island, but early development was restricted to the Active Pass area.

Henry and Sophie Georgeson arrived on Galiano in 1863 and built a cabin on the bank of a small creek flowing into what is now known as Georgeson Bay. In 1873 Georgeson pre-empted 146 acres adjacent to the bay and built a new home near White House Rock at the western entrance to Active Pass. Georgeson later moved over to Mayne to take over the new lighthouse at Georgina Point.

John O'Brien pre-empted 150 acres near Georgeson on Galiano in 1870 and the two men hunted deer on the islands and sold the meat in Victoria and New Westminster. Georgeson stood only 5' 8" but was strong and wiry, able to carry 200-pound packs in the Cariboo or two deer slung over his shoulders on Galiano.[1]

The largest early land block on Galiano was held by Henry Morris, who acquired 150 acres in the valley behind Georgeson Bay in 1873 and 1,300 acres behind the south-end bluffs three years later where he ran sheep.

Harry Clapham, a former seaman, pre-empted 160 acres in the valley in 1873. He built his cabin a mile inland because he was afraid of Indian marauders on the shoreline. A bachelor, Clapham lived a solitary existence with his dog Nellie on the little farm he carved out of the bush.

First to settle near the northern end was John Shaw, who arrived from England in 1877 with his wife and three children at a little bay that became known as Shaw's Landing. Mail came once a month, carried across Salt Spring from Vesuvius and rowed across Trincomali Channel by an Indian. When steamers began stopping offshore, Shaw would row out for mail and groceries. On summer Sundays he rowed over to Salt Spring for church services in Thomas Griffiths's home. The Shaws rowed to Nanaimo, the nearest commercial centre, for supplies.[2]

At the turn of the century the seaman-adventurer John Claus Voss boarded at the Shaw house while working on a 50-year-old Nootka dugout canoe which he had bought and named the *Tilikum*. John Shaw Jr., a bachelor who lived with his by-then widowed mother building model sailboats and tending an apple orchard, helped Voss outfit the little vessel. They added a cabin, decking, a 300-pound keel, three masts and two water-tight bulkheads. The hull was strengthened with an oak frame, floor boards were put in, and the gunwales built up seven inches. The work was carried out at an adjacent little bay, Spotlight Cove, under the supervision of boatbuilder Harry Vollmers. After Mrs. Vollmers had sewn the sails, the *Tilikum*, which would later circumnavigate the globe in an epic voyage, had her first trials along the Galiano shoreline.[3]

A neighbour of the Shaws was Captain Edward McCoskrie, a flute-playing sea captain who became a landlubber at Retreat Cove, just south of Shaw's Landing, in 1894. McCoskrie died in 1925 at Prince Rupert, where he was harbour master, but the 160-acre

Galiano property was held by this family for the next 85 years.

Charles Groth, a Danish-born seaman who had jumped ship at Victoria in 1875 at 21, arrived on Galiano in 1880 after marrying 16-year-old Elizabeth Georgeson, one of Henry's daughters. The couple lived on the Georgeson property for a year until Groth pre-empted 160 acres next to O'Brien's land. They built a new house which was completed by the end of 1882. Groth had worked for a time as a farmhand for Noah Buckley on North Pender Island before setting out on his own with a small flock of sheep. Each sheep-owner in the area placed a distinctive coal-tar mark on his animals, which were allowed to roam the island at large until shearing time. There were frequent losses to cougars and rustlers.[4]

Groth steadily expanded the size of his farm, growing vegetables and starting an apple orchard. To protect his market-bound crops from the island's prolific deer population, he built extensive cedar-rail fences and used his rifle. In 1882 he recorded shooting 24 deer, which provided extra meat for the table and hides which were tanned for sale in Victoria and New Westminster.

As his family grew with the births of six children, Groth found extra work on Galiano roads and two government projects on Mayne—the lighthouse and the new wharf at Miners Bay, built in 1885. In August 1888, Groth paid the $160 pre-emption fee to gain full title to his property.

Finlay Murcheson with his wife and son took land fronting Whaler Bay on the southeast shore of the island in 1882 and hacked a homestead out of the timber and brush. Mrs. Murcheson was the first white woman to settle on the island. Her husband in subsequent years became road foreman, fire warden and school trustee.

Whaler Bay, which had been used as a shelter by small whaling vessels in the strait, was protected by 80-acre Gossip Island. The island was owned first by Henry Morris in 1884 and was sold in 1921 to Captain I.G. Denroche, who had operated a sawmill there during the war with his sons. Denroche built a resort after buying the island, but gave up in a few years because of the lack of boat service and became the owner-operator of the nine-hole golf course on Galiano.

Mr. and Mrs. Finlay Murcheson. (COURTESY BC ARCHIVES)

A pioneer in the Whaler Bay area was Robert Anthony Wright from Belfast, who settled in the 1870s. In 1896, after his first wife died, he married Isabel Trueworthy, who would row from Galiano to Orcas Island in the San Juans, a distance of almost 30 miles, to visit her mother. Isabel "Belle" and her brother William "Billy" had been brought up on Mayne by Mrs. William Robson. Their father, William Trueworthy, was the brother of Charles Trueworthy, Saturna's first settler. William died young, and when his wife remarried, Belle and Billy rebelled against the stepfather and were moved to Mayne. Isabel died at 30 giving birth to her fifth child in 1906, and Wright was drowned on New Year's Day, 1914, while rowing across from Mayne to Otter Bay on Pender in his small boat.

Another old-timer in that area was William Cain, an English-born carpenter and cabinet-maker who bought the land south of Whaler Bay that became known as the Cain Peninsula; he built a house there in 1894 that contained ornate hand-carved woodwork.

The first schoolhouse had been built in the south-end valley in 1892. John Georgeson's children walked five miles to the school from Montague Harbour, which they crossed by boat to reach the trailhead.

Galiano settlers for many years rowed across the pass to Miners Bay to shop. They did not get their own store until 1903. Yorkshireman Joseph Burrill had arrived on Galiano in 1896 and acquired 80 acres of waterfront at the eastern entrance to Active Pass. In 1899 he was joined by his brother Fred and they farmed together for four years until they opened the store, with Joe in charge. The back room is still a gathering place for islanders today.

There was a Swiss cowbell over the door which customers could ring at any time for service. Large orders such as sacks of flour or chicken feed were delivered around the south end of the island by Joe. He used a team of oxen at first, then a horse and buggy. Later the Burrills added a post office, library and gasoline pumps for fishermen, and their establishment became the island's social centre. A store and coffee shop still serve that function today, moved to a new location with a false front added.

Fred Burrill was shy, while Joe was a convivial man who liked to stop for tea and a chat when delivering groceries. He gave little bags of candy or an "all-day sucker" to children who came into the store. Joe thought nothing of rowing 13 miles to Pender to play grass hockey, then rowing home again at night. Life-long bachelors— Fred did the cooking and gardening, made furniture and ran the farm—both Burrills were keen musicians. Joe played the piano, while Fred strummed banjo, guitar, violin and piano and had a strong tenor voice. On musical evenings at the Burrill home overlooking the pass, the Georgesons joined in with violins. Peter Georgeson played the accordion for dances.

For some years Edmund Buckley, son of an English landowner, lived in a little apartment over the Burrills' store. Buckley was working on one of the island roads when word reached him that his father had died. He turned down a knighthood, but his son later accepted it.

Joe Burrill's musical talents were partly responsible for bringing another pioneer family to Galiano. Alexander Scoones had been a seaman after leaving his home in England; during a Victoria stopover in 1897 he decided to return ashore for good. When he entered the lobby of the Dallas Hotel, Scoones was entranced by the sight and sound of the desk clerk sitting on the counter strumming a guitar. The musician was Joe Burrill, over from his Galiano place to make some money before the arrival of his brother. Burrill did such a selling job on the beauties of Galiano that Scoones decided to have a look. He promptly purchased six acres of Burrill's property at Mary Anne Point, taking over a cottage there for the next three years.

Scoones began fishing off the mouth of the Fraser in a rowboat with gillnet and sail, often making the 30-mile return trip to Galiano on summer weekends. In 1900 he returned to England to resume his engineering studies, and then spent a number of years in Brazil before the war. In 1919 he returned to the cottage with his older brother Paul, and a year later sent to England for Edith Olliff to come and be his bride.

Paul, who remained a bachelor, was one of Galiano's most respected residents. A former mathematics teacher at Eton College, he was a school trustee and justice of the peace. He brought out a splendid library of books and records, and musical evenings with the Scoones were a highlight of early social life on the island. Indeed, every night was open house for music lovers. Paul had a gramophone that used bamboo needles. Edith Scoones was an accomplished singer and participant in these affairs. Alex was 76 when he died in 1952, while Paul died in Victoria at the age of 87.

As on Mayne, some of the early settlers had been brought together in the various gold rushes of the last century. Edward Winstanley had come to Galiano in 1890 and bought land at Arbutus Point at the east end of Active Pass. He helped build the first school. On one of his forays to the Yukon, Winstanley became a friend of Phillip Steward and sold him a portion of his property. Steward arrived at his new homesite in 1900, and his wife and two small children followed soon after. The Stewards later moved inland to a farm in the valley. A daughter, Nesta, married Mayne's "Tomato King," Richard Hall.

Max Enke was a successful Manchester-born entrepreneur who left his rabbit-fur business in Belgium to seek a new life in B.C. He

Alex (left) and Paul Scoones, at Mary Anne Point, 1940. (COURTESY SCOONES FAMILY)

arrived at the Georgeson Bay wharf aboard the *Iroquois* in May 1907, accompanied by 11 Belgian farm workers—nine men and two women. After looking around at the available properties, Enke purchased Seabrook Farm, the ranch begun by pioneer Harry Clapham. He added three adjacent properties, bringing his holdings to 1,300 acres.

After getting the property, which he called "Valley Farm", into operation, Enke returned to Montreal to marry Marion, the daughter of a wealthy family, who had studied English literature at Cambridge. Marion's mother had accompanied her across the Atlantic for the wedding. Max had to satisfy the family that he had proper accommodation for Marion in the wilds of western Canada before the marriage was approved. Not only did Max have a suitable place for his bride, he bought a fancy four-wheeled, two-horse carriage in Victoria to drive her about. In 1910 a daughter, Ruth, became the first white child born on the island. Despite the amenities her husband had provided, Marion Enke found the country life constraining and the family moved in 1913 to a big house overlooking the

Marion Enke. (COURTESY BC ARCHIVES)

water in Oak Bay in Victoria. The Enkes later donated 336 acres of land for Bluffs Park above Georgeson Bay.[5]

Another park donor on Galiano was the Bellhouse family. J. Wortley Bellhouse arrived on the island from Manitoba in 1907 with his wife and six children. He bought the property of Robert Grubb, who had started farming about 1890 at the south end of Sturdies Bay. Grubb had built up a herd of Jersey cattle and Bellhouse expanded his dairy business. His cattle, named after characters in the works of his beloved Charles Dickens, won many prizes at farm fairs on Vancouver Island and the mainland. Bellhouse's son Leonard took over the property in 1921 and ran the Farmhouse Inn. Leonard's wife Jessie was a granddaughter of the provincial attorney-general, Henry Crease.

Stanley and Dorothy Page, starting out in 1912, lived all of their 60-year married life in the same house on a 70-acre ranch. As newlyweds they rowed across to Mayne for dances. Mrs. Page said the early Galiano settlers enjoyed a "genteel" kind of pioneering, unlike the harsh life on the prairies. They didn't worry about missing a day's work to enjoy a social function. It became harder to live off the land, however, when the big snowfall of 1916 killed off the pheasants and grouse. (Logging had taken away the birds' winter forest cover.) Groceries were ordered from New Westminster or Victoria. The Pages had an apple orchard, cattle, pigs, chickens and sheep. When farming became uneconomic Stan took up carpentry and other jobs, such as running a taxi service, to help pay the bills. At the age of 89 he was the oldest registered taxi driver in Canada.

By the turn of the century there was still only a rough "cow trail" running the 18 miles between the south and north ends of the island. Settlers with messages or small packages for the Porlier Pass area would pin instructions with an axe left on a stump at the start of the path for anyone headed that way on horseback or by foot.

The twin lighthouses at Porlier Pass, separating Galiano from Valdes Island and sometimes known as Cowichan Gap or simply "The Gap," were completed in 1902. The two lights were at Race Point and Virago Point, which was reachable only by boat. Their keeper was Frank "Sticks" Allison, a seaman who had run away from home in Scotland at the age of nine in 1875 and joined his uncle on a sailing ship. He arrived in B.C. by way of Glace Bay, Nova Scotia, where he had worked in the coal mines. Allison took up the same occupation in Nanaimo until he damaged a hip in an underground explosion in 1901. As he hobbled around the hospital on crutches, Allison befriended a little boy who described him as "the man with the sticks," and the nickname stuck. He was still using the crutches when he began at the lighthouse but later exchanged them for a cane.[6]

Sticks and his bride Matilda, a granddaughter of Henry Georgeson, were forced to live at first in a little lean-to shack left behind by the carpenters who built the lights. They hauled water in pails from a stream until a 400-gallon rainwater tank was installed. Passing boats used to throw newspapers into the water for Sticks to retrieve in his small boat and dry out beside the stove. Until a post office was established at Shaw's Landing in 1912, Allison rowed over to Kuper Island for mail twice a month.

Allison had no foghorn in the early years and his daughter Devina Baines later recalled: "In the foggy weather, when he would hear the boats blowing out in the Gulf or out in the channel, he'd get himself up on the top of the hill where the sound would travel, and get an old coal-oil tin and a stick and he used to beat away on this tin can to show the boats as they came closer where the pass was."[7]

Devina and her sister Frances both married lightkeepers who took over the Porlier lights when Allison retired in 1941 after 39 years' service. Though short, Porlier Pass is one of the most difficult channels in the islands to navigate. Tides reach nine knots, and rips and whirlpools are a constant hazard. Over the years the Allisons fed and warmed dozens of victims of the swirling currents off Race Point. Despite the heavy volume of traffic through the pass—as many as 121 tugs with tows and 80 steamships in a month—there were few major mishaps. One was the sinking in September 1923 of the tug *Peggy McNeil* with the loss of five men. It was a calm night but there was a strong tide running when the tug rolled over and sank after becoming fouled in the towline to two barges. One crewman survived.

John Peter, once an Indian chore boy for the Hudson's Bay Company's James Douglas, later became chief of a Cowichan band at the north end of Galiano. He gave approval for a marine service station on reserve land at the pass which was operated for 19 years by Elizabeth Allison, another daughter of Sticks.

There were also a number of Japanese around Porlier engaged in fishing. At times as many as a hundred boats worked the pass for cod. These craft were from 25 to 35 feet long, with an engine and long oars. There were little cabins fore and aft, and wives and children lived aboard. The Japanese also seined in the pass for herring which, with the cod, were treated in salt-brine vats. There were five "saltery" buildings on Galiano, four run by Japanese and the other by Chinese workers. Some Indians worked in the Japanese salteries, which were built over the water on pilings, with bunkhouses at the back on the shore. After being soaked in the brine, the herring were shipped to China in 400-pound boxes. The Japanese built a new saltery at Retreat Cove just before the war but it was abandoned when they were evacuated. A herring cannery suffered the same fate.[8]

A number of Galiano settlers took on "outside" jobs to earn a bit of money during times of economic recession. Crawford Twiss and his wife rented a cottage from Max Enke for $2.50 a month. "You could live on so little and really enjoy it," Mrs. Twiss later recalled. Her husband began working for Burrills' store making deliveries, as well as putting in time on the roads. For four months every summer for 30 years he went north to work at the A.B.C. Cannery on the Skeena River. His neighbour on Galiano, Henry W. Harris, was the cannery manager.

For wives required to stay at home during such periods to look after children and farms, there was often "shack fever" to contend with. Mrs. Twiss recalled that sometimes in the months of the year when her husband was working on their property, she would join other wives in travelling to nearby islands for dances. The men, tired after a hard day in the fields, stayed home and looked after the children. When they felt similarly cooped up, the husbands would occasionally row to one of the islands for a game of bridge. Mrs. Twiss described Galiano as "very British and very conservative."[9]

Politics were often lively on the islands. After the owner of the steamship *Iroquois*, Thomas W. Paterson, won a provincial byelection in 1902 for Victoria North riding, which included Sidney and the southern Gulf Islands, accusations of voting irregularity were laid. Philip Robinson, a longshoreman known on the Vancouver waterfront as "Brockey Phil," was charged with bringing skid-road drifters from Vancouver to impersonate voters at the Galiano Island poll and vote for Paterson. They were paid five dollars apiece. The bogus voters were transported on the *Iroquois*.

Someone, presumably Paterson, had ordered Captain William Beynon to cancel the *Iroquois*'s regular return run from Nanaimo to Sidney via the islands and travel to Vancouver. It arrived at the Evans Coleman dock there at three A.M. on election day, December 23, to take on 24 men rounded up by Robinson. Most were roused from their beds in the Europa Hotel, where rooms were thoughtfully provided by Robinson to ensure their departure. Each was handed a slip of paper with the name of an eligible voter in Sidney whom they were to impersonate at the Galiano polling station.

The *Iroquois* arrived at Sturdies Bay at eight A.M. and stayed a few hours while the men sauntered off in ones and twos to vote before being returned to Vancouver. Sure enough, when the Galiano votes were tallied Paterson had out-polled his opponent 34 to 17, helping him to a 196-153 victory in the riding.

At Robinson's trial skipper Beynon and purser William Macro were reluctant witnesses. Macro said because the trip was a "special charter" the passengers paid no fares and there was no list of names. Neither would disclose the identity of the man who ordered them to make the unusual voyage, but only Paterson had that power. Fortunately for him the judge ruled that the question did not have to be answered because it did not bear on the guilt or innocence of Robinson, the only man charged. Robinson was convicted, fined $400 and sent to jail for a year. Paterson emerged unscathed from the scandal and later was rewarded for his political acumen by being named Lieutenant-Governor of the province.

In the 1940s and '50s Galiano became a beacon for the other Gulf Islands in the provision of electrical power. There were a number of costly individual power generators on the island when the residents got together to form the Galiano Light and Power Company. Fred Robson, owner of the Galiano Lodge, was the sparkplug for the project, donating a 600-hp diesel engine. Poles were supplied by logging operator Ollie Garner and others. One qualified electrician and an experienced lineman contributed their skills. Workbees were held on Sundays, with the wives putting up a picnic lunch.

The first power was switched on after the final connection had been made on December 8, 1949. That initial system served only three guest lodges and the Garner home, but the power co-op was on its way. The following week two more homes and Jack's Coffee Bar were hooked up, and new connections followed steadily. A ceremonial opening of the system was held in July 1950, with Premier Byron Johnson throwing the switch. The work of running the company was done on a voluntary basis, except for $40 a month paid to a maintenance man. Assisted by his wife Edith, Alex Scoones was secretary-treasurer and meter-reader until his death in 1952. As the company expanded, it became necessary to hire a full-time staff, until the government-run B.C. Power Commission took over the operation in 1956. The Galiano service thus became the first link in extension of electrical power to the islands.

In more recent years Galiano has become known as a haven for artists and writers, mostly women. Octogenarian artist Elizabeth "Hoppy" Hopkins was the doyen of the group, which included writers Jane Rule, Audrey Thomas and Dorothy Livesay. Individualists all, they did not form an artists' colony as such, but were supportive of one another.

One of Galiano's feisty women was Jean Lockwood, who in middle age started up the *Gulf Islander* newspaper in the 1960s. Among other irritations, she upset the R.C.M.P. by printing homemade wine recipes and was reprimanded for her labours. Brewing their own refreshments was nothing new for the islanders. Just after the turn of the century a well-known bootlegger's still was built on Whisky Creek running into Sturdies Bay.

Settlement on Galiano was limited in the 19th century by the lack of farming land and a shortage of water; agriculture has never been a big part of the island's economy. The population remained steady at about 300 for 60 years until development spurted in the 1970s. It is still under a thousand today and half of this number are retirees, which means the service industries are the backbone of the economy. The majority of the residents live around the southern end, where settlement of the island began.

Sheep, "Old Jack" and a Coal Mine

Away from the main steamer routes and, like Galiano, possessing little desirable land for farming, Saturna Island was late and slow to develop. It was considered so remote that Royal Navy vessels used the east-side bluffs for cannon target practice as late as 1895.

In 1872 William Elford took up land at Winter Cove on the northeast corner of the island. Elford was joined by his brother Theo. The main occupation of these first arrivals on the thin soil was sheep-raising, as it would continue to be for those who followed. Most of the sheep went to the Victoria market.

In 1873 Charles Trueworthy acquired 1,400 acres on the west side of the island facing Plumper Sound and South Pender Island. Trueworthy and his brother William had come to Canada together from Wales, and William settled on Orcas Island in the San Juans. Charles stayed on Saturna until 1884 when he moved to California seeking relief from debilitating asthma. Before his departure Trueworthy sold more than half his property—784 acres—for $5,000 to a pair of recent arrivals from Britain: Warburton Pike and Charles Payne.

Payne was a member of a wealthy English family and had been retired from the navy for a year before coming to B.C. Payne and Pike, who also came from a well-to-do family, built a house and planted some fruit trees. The two men ordered a luxurious 48-foot steam launch from a Victoria boatbuilder which was intended for pleasure cruising. On her completion early in 1886 the *Colonist* described the *Saturna* as "a shapely little thing," capable of ten knots with a 25-hp steam engine, and "fitted with every view to internal comfort." Less than three years later she was put up for sale, probably because Payne had decided to return to England. The *Saturna* finished her days mundanely as a fish packer on the Skeena River.[1]

In 1886 Payne had made a trip home and returned with his younger brother Gerald. Charles Payne had bought other properties in the Gulf Islands and Victoria area, but lived most of his life in England. In addition to the Saturna property, Pike and Charles Payne had also bought nine acres of land in Oak Bay from Trueworthy for $30 an acre.

Warburton Pike stands out as one of the most remarkable of the Gulf Islands men. A larger-than-life figure, he was constantly on the move. Although he spent only brief sojourns on Saturna, he made a lasting impact there, as well as on Mayne and Pender and some of the smaller islands. In between he explored the Arctic barren lands and wrote books about his adventures, promoted a northern B.C. mining property and railway, and was involved in a number of business ventures. While he was away from the ranch, he left John Wessel in charge. Wessel had worked for James Alexander on Pender before hiring on with Pike.

Born in Dorsetshire, England, in 1861, Pike attended Rugby School and graduated from Oxford. He was the youngest son and, as was often the custom, left the estate to go abroad. Before picking Saturna as a place to set down roots for a time, Pike had been an explorer in Iceland, cowboy in Wyoming, miner in California and Oregon, and hunter on the Canadian prairies. He was by turns reserved, cynical, generous, amusing, offhand and modest, a man most comfortable alone in the wilds. Yet he was "one of the most courteous of men. . . liked by everybody." He was described as "a mysterious and romantic character [who] would simply disappear without a word and then appear back without a word." He was a man's man, but women were attracted by his aura of mystery. His drooping moustache and large nose gave him a taciturn, almost morose appearance, but his face was otherwise fine-featured.[2]

Pike enjoyed roughing it in the bush and declared that "the best place to sleep is under a tree." Even after building a comfortable house on Saturna, he liked to sleep under a large maple on the property. Pike's home was a popular gathering spot for his bachelor friends and the Payne, Spalding, Grey and Higgs families of Saturna and Pender. Cricket was a favourite pastime on the field.

After Charles Payne had gone back to his Bedfordshire home to look after family affairs, his brother Gerry stayed on with Pike. Other Payne brothers and sisters followed to take up residence on Saturna.

l. to r. Ralph Grey, Edward Winstanley, Gerry Payne, Fred Robson.
(COURTESY BC ARCHIVES)

In his first diary entry Gerry Payne recalled arriving on Saturna in 1886: "I was put to sleep in the fruit shed, on a shelf among the apples and straw. Mr. Pike gave me a great-coat and I rolled up in it. The stars shone bright through the cracks in the wall, the cats fought and screeched all night under the house, and I could hear the men playing cards through the wall. The place smelled like cider. It was my sixteenth birthday."[3]

After his brother had left, Gerry Payne lived on Pike's ranch for six years before pre-empting 900 acres of his own around Boot Cove and building a frame house at Breezy Bay. He was helped on the property by John "Old Jack" Blantern, who stayed with Payne for 40 years. Blantern milked the cows and cared for the horses but avoided the pigs and chickens, which he did not like. A bachelor, Blantern had a little log house on the property decorated with pictures of glamorous, cinch-waisted Victorian women cut out from magazines and calendars. In his spare time he carved little wooden knick-knacks such as whistles, and gave haircuts. A hard drinker, he went off to Victoria on week-long binges. Back on the island he would buy a bottle from the legendary Billy Trueworthy.

Billy, the son of William Trueworthy and his Indian wife, was a nephew of Charles. He lived in a little shack Pike had built for him, herding and shearing sheep. He was described as small and slight with "the most beautiful eyes like brown velvet with kind of a sparkle in them." Billy was very quiet except when he was rounding up sheep. Then he would let out a yell "high wild and fierce" that echoed over the Saturna hills. "The dogs would all crouch on the ground; they couldn't stand it." Another islander, Constance (Grey) Swartz said Billy "ran as fast or faster than any dog... he'd streak up and down Prairie Hill on Saturna... just like a wild animal in the bush." Mrs. Swartz said Billy was loved by everybody, but that was not quite true. The Payne family could never quite forgive him for his bootlegging activities and supplying Jack Blantern with cheap liquor.[4]

The next Payne to arrive was Harold, who had spent five years sailing around the world as a cadet, starting at the age of 15. He landed on Saturna in 1891 and proceeded to build a combined store and post office. Until that time the settlers had rowed three miles

Billy Trueworthy. (COURTESY BC ARCHIVES)

across Plumper Sound to Corbett's Store—"General Merchandise, Flour, Feed Etc."—at Hope Bay on North Pender.

There was no steamship service yet to Saturna, and Payne rowed across to Mayne once a week to pick up the mail. Harold sold the store after a time and bought farming land at Winter Cove, but soon dropped that to join Pike in his northern ventures. In 1906, after his return from the Boer War, Harold married Ruth Kathleen Maude of Mayne, daughter of Eustace and Grace Maude of the old Point Comfort Hotel, and went back to farming. Following the death of his wife, Payne was married in 1916 to Jessie Ryall. They moved to Oak Bay so their five children could go to high school. A son, Reg, later became president of the United Fishermen and Allied Workers Union. A move to North Saanich followed, where Harold was near his sister Polly, who had married George Bradley-Dyne, an old friend of Gerry Payne's in England.

Bradley-Dyne had bought a farm in Saanich from Dr. J.S. Helmcken in 1906 and two years later acquired Pike's Saturna property. The Bradley-Dynes raised prize dogs, sheep, horses and pigeons, and ran the store and post office at Saturna Beach for a time, before moving back to Vancouver Island. The original Pike property, reduced to about 900 acres from the original 1,400, had a number of owners over the years. It has been the site of the annual July 1 lamb barbecue which draws hundreds of visitors to Saturna. The event was begun in 1950 by Jim Cruickshank as an annual school picnic. Cruickshank had learned the "Argentine style" of cooking meat in Patagonia. The barbecue was continued and expanded by the new owners of the Pike property, Jim and Lorraine Campbell.

In 1912 Pike bought 160 acres on the south half of Discovery Island off Victoria's Cadboro Bay and built a house. When war broke out in 1914 he went off to England to enlist. Depressed when he was rejected, Pike had a nervous breakdown and committed suicide at a seaside nursing home only ten miles from his birthplace. A memorial cairn was erected by friends at Dease Lake. Captain Ernest Beaumont bought the Discovery Island property from Pike's estate in 1918 and lived there for the next 50 years. After his death in 1967 at 91 it became a park.

Another Payne brother, Hubert, Harold's twin, visited Saturna in the 1890s and returned in 1902 to stay. A graduate of Cambridge, Hubert had entered the ministry and was ordained at St. Paul's Cathedral. Another Payne, Isabel, followed her brothers to B.C. and kept house for Hubert for a time on Saturna. Neither married. Isabel, a noted beauty, was a free-spirited wanderer who spent much of her time sketching and painting. A rumoured romance with Pike never developed. She had a log house at Kye Bay near Comox and would drive up the island alone in a horse-drawn buggy, camping by the side of the road.[5]

With the help of Bradley-Dyne, Hubert converted an abandoned Japanese boathouse at Winter Cove into a little church which could seat 20. It was called St. Christopher's, but was never consecrated. Today it still stands as a private chapel. Hubert, who also held monthly services on Pender, was later made a canon and took over a church in Oak Bay before moving to Saanich. Harold and Hubert celebrated their 80th birthday together in 1951. Harold died three years later but Hubert lived until 1963.

Gerry Payne, meanwhile, after some adventuring in the north

with Pike, had married in 1899. His wife, Elizabeth Finnerty of San Francisco, had trained as a nurse in California. The family lived in the style that old-country money allowed, with a Chinese cook and a governess for their three girls and a boy. Nevertheless, Gerry was the most egalitarian member of the Paynes, mixing easily with people other than the English, to whom others in the family mostly confined themselves.

The only time the Paynes came close to living off the land was during the First World War when their funds were temporarily cut off. Even then it was a bit of a lark, with the children collecting starfish for fertilizer and being paid 50¢ per hundred. Ham, bacon and salmon were cured in a smokehouse. Apples from the orchard were shipped to Ladner by scow.

In 1887 Pike sold a portion of his property at East Point to the federal government for a lighthouse. Demands for a light had mounted the previous year after the big barque *John Rosenfeld* ran aground on Boiling Reef below the point; she was being towed by a tug out to the winds of Juan de Fuca Strait with the largest shipment of coal ever made from Nanaimo. She was bound for San Francisco when the mishap occurred on a misty February day. The sails, rigging and fittings were removed from the vessel but the wreckage remained on the rocks, with some of the coal ending up in Saturna stoves.[6]

As early as 1861 Captain G.H. Richards of the Royal Navy had warned that three-mile-wide Boundary Pass was a dangerous waterway and ships should stay in mid-channel. Surveying the area in H.M.S. *Plumper*, Richards found tide rips, races and a flood tide from Rosario Strait that pushed vessels toward East Point. Currents swept past the point at up to seven knots.[7]

The Americans began constructing a light on Patos Island on the other side of the pass at the same time, and the East Point beacon, 120 feet above the sea, began flashing in 1888. After a temporary keeper had been in charge for a year, the station was taken over by Henry Georgeson's brother James, recently arrived from the Shetlands with his wife and five children. Mrs. Georgeson was the first white woman to settle on Saturna, where four more children were born to the family. Peter Georgeson was the first white child born on the island in 1891.

As the children grew up James wanted them to have a proper education, so he maintained a cottage for them on property he owned near the school on Mayne. He put his oldest children in charge. Later, some of them went to high school in Victoria. Andrew Georgeson built and operated the first sawmill on Saturna for Gerry Payne at Boot Cove in 1916, and built small boats. He was the manager of the fish-reduction plant on Pender, as well as working at times as an engineer at the Skeena River salmon canneries. Andrew married the daughter of Len and Emma Higgs of Pender.

James also worked his Mayne property as a part-time farm, leaving a daughter in charge of the light. His annual salary was only $480 a year, less than half the wage paid to a Chinese workman who cleared the land for the station when it was built. Georgeson sailed twice a year to New Westminster to pick up basic food supplies at prices cheaper than on the islands.[8]

In 1909 Georgeson suffered a stroke and his son Peter took over the light until his father retired in 1921. At that time Peter officially took charge and remained there until 1939, when he transferred to the Albert Head lighthouse, ending the family's 52-year residence at East Point. James died on Saturna in 1926 at 79; his wife was 93 when she died in hospital at Ganges in 1949.

Peter Georgeson in 1920 had married the daughter of John Aitken of Mayne. Later she recalled gathering rainwater in cisterns at the lighthouse for drinking, with only a few gallons left over for cleaning: "We had to wash the clothes and wash the kids and wash the floors and wash the dog all in that, and then put it back on the garden." Schooling for the children was the main motive for moving to Albert Head, she said. Peter, who had become an expert boat-builder at East Point, completed 80 small boats at his new station to help pay the bills.[9]

TUMBO ISLAND

Lying off the southeast shore of Saturna is 260-acre, boomerang-shaped Tumbo Island. The earliest resident, Ike Tatton, witnessed a large-scale battle between warring Indian tribes on the island. In later years, human skulls and bones found scattered over a wide area on the shore indicated that many were killed. Tatton climbed a tall tree for safety and a vantage point while the battle raged.

Small coal deposits had been discovered on Saturna before the turn of the century, but none proved large enough for commercial development. In the 1890s a major effort was made on Tumbo, again without success. Spearheading the project was Charles Gabriel, who had been running a Japanese trading-goods store in Victoria. On a buying trip in Yokohama he met a dynamic young Japanese, Kisuki Mikuni, whom he persuaded to come to Canada. Mikuni worked as a clerk at the bazaar until Gabriel sold it in 1889 to form the Tumbo Island Coal Company. Mikuni was his assistant in the new endeavour.

By 1893 a shaft had been driven down 200 feet and 21 men, including a number recruited in Kyushu, Japan, were working in the mine. Two men, the contractor and an engineer, were killed that year when a boiler exploded. From that point on the project ran into continuing problems. At 245 feet water came into the shaft and work was stopped; the company folded. Work was resumed by another group in 1906, but without success. Mikuni, meanwhile, began farming on Saturna but soon moved to the mainland, where he became involved in a number of business enterprises.[10]

In 1905 a German recluse named Barnard Wenzel was living on the west side of Tumbo. On a stormy evening in October another German, John Shultz, sought shelter in the lee of the island. Wenzel warned him to keep away. The two men argued and Wenzel went to his cabin to get a gun. When he returned Shultz had a gun in his hand too. Wenzel fired first and missed. Shultz fired back in the twilight and left the scene. He was afraid Wenzel had been wounded and went to Justice of the Peace Tom Collinson on Mayne Island. Constable Angus Ego set out immediately in the early hours of October 14 and rowed miles in rough weather to Tumbo, making the voyage in just three hours. On the doorstep of Wenzel's cabin the constable found the hermit dead of a gunshot wound. No action was taken against Shultz.[11]

* * *

Although Saturna never did deliver its promised coal, sandstone became an important export. Pike started a quarry on his property which flourished with the arrival from England of stonemason George Taylor. After landing on the island in 1892 with his wife and five children, Taylor pre-empted land at Potato Bay on Plumper Sound where he built a two-storey sandstone house, but soon went to work at his trade for Pike. The site of the quarry, close by Potato Bay, became known as Taylor Point.

The quarry produced building stone used in Victoria for the Armouries, Public Library, Craigdarroch Castle, Metropolitan Church and the caps on the gate pillars at Royal Roads Military College. A considerable quantity of stone was also shipped to Winnipeg and other prairie centres. To load the blocks of stone, tugs moved scows up to the shore where there was a deepwater drop-off.

At the turn of the century there were a large number of Japanese-Canadian fishermen operating out of Winter Cove, but few permanent settlers. Two families living at the north end of the island made a living cutting cordwood for greenhouses and canneries in Ladner.

In the summer of 1889 Mrs. Joseph W. McKay, wife of the Hudson's Bay Company factor, had brought their four "high-spirited" daughters to Saturna from Victoria for a holiday as guests of Warburton Pike. The eldest, Agnes, was engaged to Pike at the time, but the marriage was called off. Pike remained a bachelor. A second daughter, Lilias, returned in November to be married to Arthur Reed Spalding in Pike's ranch-house. After the wedding, performed by Canon Beanlands, they were paddled by Indians across Plumper Sound to Spalding's South Pender Island home in a big canoe hired by the father of the bride.

SAMUEL ISLAND

One of Pike's bachelor friends was Ralph Geoffrey Grey, known to his friends as "R.G." or "Archie." He was a relative of Earl Grey, Governor General of Canada from 1904 to 1911, but from a poorer side of the family. (Later in life Ralph dabbled in socialist theories.) A daughter, Constance "Conti" Grey, said her father had been "kicked out" of his family home at Pilston Hall, Northumberland, "by a wicked stepmother."[12]

Grey came to Victoria with a friend from Ireland, George Rutherford, and the two men bought 470-acre Samuel Island between Mayne and Saturna. The 200-yard-wide channel between Samuel and Saturna is known as Canoe Pass or Boat Passage. When Rutherford decided to return home, Grey became the sole owner. He built a house with verandas and fireplaces and painted it white, but it was never quite completed.

Grey kept sheep, a few head of cattle, pigs, rabbits and chickens on his property. A fence was built around the vegetable plot to keep deer out. A stand of big cedars at one end of the property was preserved until he sold the island. Unlike the neighbouring Paynes, who could pay for labourers with farm skills, Grey and other young Englishmen of limited means had to learn by trial and error how to do everything around the place. As a result, they stuck mostly to the basics of farming.

For added income Grey worked as a camp boss at a Steveston cannery in the summer months, leaving Billy Trueworthy to care for his sheep. Grey also joined Pike, Gerry and Harold Payne, Edward Winstanley and others in the Yukon and Cassiar district mining and railway ventures.

Arthur Spalding had grown up in Sussex, at Ore Place, Hastings, with the three children of his step-sister, Eliza Amelia (Spalding) Higgs. Soon after he came to B.C., Spalding was followed by one of the Higgs children, Leonard. Although he was Arthur's step-nephew, Higgs was only four years younger. After returning to England to marry Emma Batsford, Len Higgs lived for a year on Saturna and then bought land on Pender.

Higgs's sisters, Mabel and Winifred, followed him to Saturna at the turn of the century and set up a little "school" for Leonard's children. They joined in the social set that gathered at the Paynes' or at Pike's place. There Winifred met Ralph Grey and they were married by Canon Paddon at Harold Payne's house. On the afternoon of the wedding the couple forked hay that had been cut by Ralph the previous day.

A cottage called "Loggia" was built for Mabel Higgs beside Winifred and Ralph's house on Samuel. She later married Martin Grainger, B.C.'s second Chief Forester, following H.R. MacMillan, and the author of a novel which has become a minor Canadian classic, *Woodsmen of the West*, based on his experiences as a logger. Like Pike, he was one of the most accomplished and intriguing of the expatriate group whose lives were entwined on the islands.

Winifred Grey had a chronic heart condition and the family moved in 1910 to Esquimalt, where Ralph picked up odd jobs, and they also lived in Vancouver for a time. While on a pheasant-hunting expedition to Samuel Island in 1906, Earl Grey had offered Ralph a post at Government House in Ottawa but he had declined.

In later years Samuel passed into the hands of a succession of wealthy owners. They included engineer A.J.T. Taylor of Vancou-

Ralph Grey and his daughter, Constance, hauling hay with a donkey, ca *1908.* (COURTESY BC ARCHIVES)

ver, who developed the British Properties subdivision in West Vancouver for the Guinness interests, and designed and built the Lions Gate Bridge. Taylor was born in Victoria in 1887, the son of Reverend George Taylor who later moved to Nanaimo and Gabriola Island. Taylor subsequently sold Samuel Island to foodstore magnate Garfield Weston. In the 1960s and early '70s there were proposals to build two bridges linking 2 1/2-mile-long Samuel with Mayne and Saturna, but they were not acted upon.

Saturna remains the most isolated of the large islands in the southern group, with the poorest ferry service. The resident population has remained under 300, although there may be twice that number in the summer despite the absence of tourist facilities. Many of the cottages are unoccupied in the winter months. That's the way Saturna people like it. A magazine in 1990 described the character of the island as "independent, reclusive, anarchic."[13]

Politics, an Elopement
and Lady Buttercup

In the beginning there was only one island, connected by a narrow isthmus known as "the Portage." The early settlers became accustomed to dragging their small boats over this land bridge to get from Bedwell Harbour on the west to Browning Harbour on the east without tackling the sometimes treacherous waters of the south end.

Not everyone was in favour when the Dominion government in 1902 acceded to the wishes of Thomas Paterson, the influential owner of the steamship *Iroquois*, to dredge the passageway and make a canal separating Pender into North and South islands. There had always been a geographic separation between the two, but the canal made it official. A bridge spanning the canal was not built until 1955.

Although Bedwell Harbour is regarded today as one of the Gulf Islands' best anchorages, it was not always so. In the early days of working sailing ships rather than pleasure yachts, it was pointed out that a vessel seeking shelter there from a gale "would be likely to stay until a fair wind came in order to get out again, as the entrance is too narrow to beat out."[1]

Another hazard of early times, not a threat to today's Pender Islander, was Indian violence. In 1863 one of the most publicized murders of the period occurred at Bedwell Harbour. Bill Brady, an American who had lived in Victoria for four years, was hunting in the islands with a Black companion from Texas, John Henley. Travelling in a whaleboat, the two men pitched a tent on the shore in Shark Cove at the north end of the Portage. They had a friendly exchange with five Indians camped nearby, but during the night Brady and Henley were hit by shots fired through the walls of the tent.

Brady was severely wounded, but Henley managed to get his gun and chase off the attackers. The incident happened on a Saturday night; Henley stayed until Brady died on Tuesday, then managed to row and sail to Victoria to notify authorities. Five Cowichan Indians were later arrested at Kulleet Bay near Chemainus. Three men were subsequently hanged for murder, one woman was freed, and another sentenced to life imprisonment.

This was some time before there were settlers on Pender, which was one of the last of the islands to develop because the desirable land had been tied up by a single owner. Once settlement started in the 1880s, however, the land was quickly snapped up, especially the few arable pockets.

The first landowner was former Hudson's Bay Company officer John Tod, who had retired to a 100-acre farm in Oak Bay and speculated in land like many other company men. Tod did not live on the island, buying the 1,100-acre South Pender property on behalf of his son John and son-in-law John Bowker. Bowker was an American who had farmed on San Juan Island before marrying Mary Tod and investing in land around Victoria. The two younger men ran sheep, and travelled to and from the island by sailing craft and canoe.

In 1879 the Tod-Bowker land was sold to James Alexander, a brother of the owner of Hastings Mill in Burrard Inlet. It was said that James was a heavy drinker and his family wanted him sent off to Pender because he was "troublesome." Alexander balked at such exile and made only brief visits to the island. He sold 800 acres to Arthur Spalding in 1886.[2]

In 1880 the province surveyed North and South Pender islands in quarter sections. Within five years all the fertile valleys were in private hands—some held for speculation. A few holdings were as large as 1,400 acres. It was "hard for a new settler to get a foothold on these islands."[3]

Two of the earliest arrivals on North Pender were Noah Buckley and David Hope, who started as partners with 2,500 acres between them in 1878. They split the property, with Hope taking the north end of the island and Buckley the south. A stock fence was built across the island from Shingle Bay to the head of Browning Harbour to divide their properties. Ditches were dug by Hope and Buckley in a number of locations to drain swamps created by beaver dams.

David Hope died in a hunting accident in 1882 and his property was divided between his brother Rutherford and a sister, Helen Auchterlonie, both in Scotland. Helen's husband Lawrence came first to look at the property and his wife and Rutherford followed soon after. Rutherford had been in love with a girl in Edinburgh when he came out after his brother's death, but her father refused them permission to marry. In 1895, the father died and the girl came out to wed Rutherford. He added a nursery to their cottage, but they had no children.

Buckley sold out at about the same time to Oliver Grimmer, who in turn sold the land to his brother, Washington; he had gone from his native England to Australia, where he had learned to shear sheep. Arriving in Victoria in 1877, Washington tried his luck hunting gold in the Cariboo before moving to the island in 1882. Oliver Grimmer left after his brother took over.

Washington Grimmer was North Pender's first postmaster, rowing around to Miners Bay on Mayne to get the mail from 1882 until 1891, when a small wharf was built at Port Washington so steamers could land. He married the Auchterlonies' 16-year-old daughter, Elizabeth, in 1885 and the couple had five children, three sons and two daughters, all of whom made their homes on their father's property.

The most notable arrival of a Grimmer child occurred on April 11, 1889, when Elizabeth was on her way to Mayne to be assisted by midwife Alice Bennett. She was being rowed across Navy Channel from Hope Bay toward Briggs Landing by her brother, James Auchterlonie, when the baby arrived. It was a boy, later christened Neptune "Nep" to commemorate the place of birth. Nep Grimmer's full name was widely believed to be Neptune Navy Grimmer, but Nep said he was pleased to discover later in life that it was registered only as Neptune. "I never did like 'Navy' tacked in the middle of it," he said. Nep was the second Grimmer child; in 1886 Nellie had been the first white baby born on the island.[4]

The Grimmers were active participants in island life. In 1894 Washington donated an acre of land for a community hall. After selling their house and 160 acres to Spencer Percival in 1903, the Grimmer menage moved inland to a valley where they developed a dairy cattle herd which won prizes at farm fairs in Victoria and on the mainland. In 1911, at the age of 60, Washington divided his farm among the children, then put an addition on the family home and turned it into a guest house. Ten years later he built a retirement home on the waterfront. A wiry little man who loved music and played the flute, he died in 1930 close to his 80th birthday. He was buried in the little cemetery on Mayne beside his friend Canon Paddon. Grimmer had been an ardent Anglican and was instrumental in the building of St. Peter's Church at Port Washington in 1914, on land donated by Percival. Elizabeth died in 1954 at Port Washington at the age of 76.[5]

As the eldest son, Nep Grimmer took charge of the farm. His father had sent him to the Agricultural College at Guelph, Ontario, to prepare him for farming. After the Salt Spring Island Creamery, where the Grimmers sold their dairy products for years, closed in 1954, Nep went in for beef cattle.

Spencer Percival, who had come from Manitoba with his wife in 1903, called his new Pender property "Sunny Side Ranch." He planted an orchard and in 1910 built a store near the Port Washington wharf, where he became postmaster in 1912.

Neptune Grimmer. (COURTESY BC ARCHIVES)

Before regular steamship service began at the turn of the century, the North Pender settlers kept a communal sailing sloop in a creek mouth at Hope Bay, which was used to carry livestock and produce to market at Nanaimo. Until a wharf was built at Hope Bay, the settlers rowed across to Briggs Landing on Mayne and walked to the post office at Miners Bay for mail.

Other early settlers on North Pender were the Hoosons from Yorkshire, father William and sons Evan and John. William and Evan left England first, in 1885, and Evan worked for a time on construction of the Canadian Pacific Railway, before settling on Pender with his father. Evan acquired 140 acres facing across Navy Channel to Mayne, and William took up some land between Browning Harbour and Razor Point. Evan had worked as a stonemason, bricklayer and blacksmith in England and started a quarry on his property at Hope Bay. He used the stone to build foundations, chimneys and fireplaces on the islands. Evan was also musical, and played the organ for church services in the community hall. In 1896 he married Frances "Fanny" Lawson, the first school teacher on

Pender. John Hooson joined the provincial police and moved to Rossland with his father.[6]

Also taking land at Hope Bay were brothers Robert and Sweany Colston in 1890. They were the first B.C.-born settlers on Pender. Robert was born in 1860 at Sapperton, where his father was with the Royal Engineers. When Robert Colston Sr. was appointed secretary to Governor Frederick Seymour, the family moved to Victoria. Robert Jr. worked as a foundryman in Victoria for a time, but started farming in 1880, first on Galiano and Mayne, then Pender. Sweany moved later to Mayne, but the brothers kept in close touch across the channel. When Robert's widowed mother came to live with him, she became a midwife on the island.

Another stone-cutter on Pender was Alexander Hamilton, a Scotsman who started work in Victoria for Mortimer Monumental Works Company, carving gravestones. The owner, John Mortimer, sent him in 1885 to the company's quarry at the Browning Harbour end of the Portage. Stone from the quarry was used to build the tower of Holy Trinity Cathedral in New Westminster and the sugar refinery at Vancouver. Hamilton pre-empted a quarter section at the head of the harbour, put up a cabin and cleared a few acres. In 1888 he returned to Scotland to marry Jeannie Leiper. Later the couple moved to New Westminster where Alex worked as a gravestone maker in New Westminster, but they lost their home and possessions when fire destroyed a large section of the town in 1898.

Hamilton then returned to Browning Harbour to become a farmer with his brothers Robert and Hugh. The soil around their house was largely clamshell and shale, but fruit trees flourished. When work and money were scarce on the island, Alex went to Victoria to resume his old stone-cutting trade, working on the library, the Empress Hotel and Hatley Park (later Royal Roads).

In 1890 Hamilton brought the first horse to Pender, a legendary animal named "Larry O'Brien." Hamilton purchased Larry from Reverend Robert Lennie, a pioneer Baptist minister who had been using him to make pastoral calls on the mainland, including trips over the old Yale Road to Chilliwack. In his early, glory days before being acquired by the preacher, Larry had won straightaway races down Columbia Street in New Westminster.[7]

Neighbours of Alex and Jeannie Hamilton were old friends Margaret and Alexander Brackett, who had come over from New Westminster to build the Hamiltons' house and decided to stay. Brackett was also a stone-cutter at the Taylor quarry on Saturna, and worked on the Empress. (He is said to have been angry later because the hotel allowed ivy to grow over the stone: "They might just as well have put up cement.") But Brackett was best known as "a great man with horses" who had a big wagon with a hayrack used for community hay-rides. An ingenious man, Brackett rigged up a huge bell to call in his farm workers, communicate with the Hamiltons across the bay, and ring in the new year. The children of the two families also remembered the high bar and swing which Brackett built for them. They recalled Browning Beach as a "children's heaven."[8]

Arthur Gardom had a small homestead on Razor Point, at the northeast entrance to Browning Harbour. He was a cultured man, with one of the first gramophones on the island, who made his living beachcombing logs for sawmills. One day while retrieving logs from a Mayne Island beach, he saw a pretty young woman sitting on

l. to r. Hugh Hamilton, Fred Smith, Elijah Pollard, Alex Hamilton and Harold Sutherland at the Hamiltons' farm at Browning Harbour. (COURTESY BC ARCHIVES)

the shore doing needlework. They struck up a conversation. She was Sidney Robotham, who lived with her mother and two sisters in a big house on 18 acres. Mrs. Robotham had bought the Mayne property after her husband, a former surgeon in the British army in India, had died in retirement at Duncan.

The tyrannical Mrs. Robotham was determined that her darling daughters would never marry. Few men ventured near the house. Gardom was undaunted, however, and continued to woo Sidney at secret, pre-arranged trysts. They decided to marry, and Sidney was to be packed and ready to meet Gardom when he arrived in his sailboat late on a summer's evening in August.

"While Mrs. Robotham and two of her daughters were busy at their needlework in the sitting room, Miss Sidney went to one of the outhouses to fetch her suitcase ... and made her way down the pathway to the beach." At that point the eagle-eyed mother missed Sidney and went out in the garden to look for her, "just in time to see a tall, fine-looking man helping Miss Sidney to get settled in the stern of his sailboat.

"When he saw Mrs. Robotham on the bank with her widow's veil blowing in the wind, he quickly grabbed an oar and pushed the boat away from the shore. Mrs. Robotham was shouting at the top of her voice, 'Bring back my daughter, how dare you!' Mr. Gardom, in his very loud voice replied, 'Good-bye Mother, we will be seeing you.'" Gardom and Sidney were married on Pender the next day and lived on happily. It is not recorded whether they ever reconciled with Mrs. Robotham.[9]

The first wharf on the Penders was built at Port Washington in 1891. Jim Auchterlonie got the mail for his side of the island at Hope Bay by an overland trail. His post office there was "a tiny building with a counter right across the end of it. When the postmaster brought the mail up from the boat, he leapt over the counter to the other side and sorted the mail before you and called out, 'Hamilton, Corbett, Menzies, Grimmer.' You reached out your hand for the letter."[10]

When Auchterlonie died the post office was taken over by R.S.W. Corbett, who had given up farming in Manitoba in 1901 to retire on Pender, where he saw the need for a store. He began by asking all the women on the island for their grocery lists, with their favourite brands. Putting the lists together, Corbett sent his first order to the mainland and was soon in business. The Hope Bay store prospered and expanded from groceries into hardware and farm supplies. A son, Percy, later took over the store and became active in island affairs. Two other generations of Corbetts followed in the business. The store closed in 1983, but the building is still standing.

Another expatriate Manitoba farmer was Ontario-born Albert Hugh Menzies, who moved first to New Westminster with his wife Henrietta and three young children. In 1891 they saw an advertisement in a newspaper seeking a family to work on Washington Grimmer's farm for wages, with an opportunity to acquire land. The family arrived on the steamer *Yosemite* in April of 1893. Albert lived on the island for the next 57 years until his death at 93. Menzies was a dyed-in-the-wool Liberal and Washington Grimmer was a Tory, but they put politics aside to work together. Menzies spent three years clearing land and working on the farm before Grimmer gave him a plot of uncleared land. Menzies then made a deal with Rutherford Hope for a rental lease and option to buy his 236-acre farm near the centre of the island. Hope kept five acres for a retirement home.

Menzies started on his new property with sheep, pigs, grain, vegetables and fruit trees, then went into poultry breeding on what he named the "Nob Hill Poultry Farm." His birds won numerous fall fair trophies at Victoria, Courtenay and the provincial exhibition at New Westminster. His interest turned next to Ayrshire cattle, before finally settling on Jerseys. In 1904 Menzies bought two prize Jersey cows from Robert Grubb of Galiano, who had bought a herd in Oregon and sold a number of his animals to other island farmers. Menzies's best cow, "Lady Buttercup," won first prize at the Victoria fair for the most milk and butter fat produced over a two-day period.

Menzies was assisted by his eldest son Victor, who had been eight when the family moved from the prairies. Victor lived the next 72 years on the farm, renamed "Valley Home Farm." He took the stock to the annual fairs and supervised the growing of grain for cattle feed. The Menzies also campaigned successfully to get a wharf at

Hope Bay, which brought them within a mile of steamship service to get their produce to Sidney and the train into Victoria.[11]

Andrew Angus Davidson arrived on the island in 1892 and bought 300 acres from Washington Grimmer at Clam Bay on the north shore midway between Hope Bay and Port Washington. Davidson was a legendary rower. He and Grimmer would sometimes row to Sidney, walk into Victoria and then return within 24 hours. Davidson later performed the same feat with his sons, Tom and Andrew.

Glasgow-born Robert Roe was an engineer on the C.P.R. coastal steamers and decided he wanted to settle on the Gulf Islands. He acquired land in the middle of North Pender in 1896, farmed for a time, and in 1907 bought property on the south side of Otter Bay. In 1919 he put an advertisement in the *Vancouver Province* offering a cottage for rent for the summer. Roe got one reply, from the Gordon Gray family of Vancouver, and the Roe family's career as resort operators was launched. A number of cabins were added and the holiday spot was named "Roesland." Roe's son, Robert Jr., later took it over.

Robert Jr. recalled that North Pender was split in the early days, with bitter wrangling between the Liberal side of the island around Hope Bay and the other staunchly Conservative side at Port Washington. Each faction had its own wharf and public hall. There was also a tinge of politics in the fighting between Hope Bay and Port Washington over the site of the post office.

Scottish-born John M. McDonald was yet another refugee from Manitoba winters when he arrived on Pender in 1894 with his wife Jessie and five children. He picked a 22-acre property in the valley near the home of his sister, Mrs. Albert Menzies. Three more children were born to them on the island and eight were too many mouths to feed from the stump ranch McDonald had cleared. He got work off the island, using his expertise as an axe-man to build bridges in remote areas. He died in 1918 at age 74, but Jessie lived on to 1953 and was 93 when she died.

In 1894 the first school board was elected on the island, made up of Andrew Davidson, James Auchterlonie and Albert Menzies, who held the post of secretary-treasurer for the next 20 years. There were

11 pupils that first year: three Davidsons, two Grimmers, three Menzies and three McDonalds. The first classes were held in the community hall, mid-way on the road between Hope Bay and Port Washington, before an adjacent schoolhouse was built in 1894.

In 1913 Mrs. Jeannie Hamilton ran for school trustee against a bachelor, Elijah Pollard. It was the first time on the islands that a woman had run for public office, and that created a stir. The Bible was quoted by both sides in support of their candidacy. Mrs. Hamilton lost. It was probably no coincidence that 1913 marked the first large-scale protests in the province by the women's suffrage movement. A petition containing 10,000 names demanding the vote was summarily dismissed by the Conservative government of Richard McBride. Women did not get the ballot in B.C. elections until 1917, when the Liberals had taken over in Victoria.

There was little industry on the island, but a herring- and dogfish-reduction plant opened at Shingle Bay in 1927, providing employment for 15 to 20 men in the summer months. Lubricating oil was extracted from the fish and the dry residue sacked and sold as fertilizer. The machinery was run by electricity generated below a lake in the interior of the island. There was some bunkhouse accommodation but most of the workers lived on the island. Andrew Georgeson was the manager of the plant, which ran until it burned down in 1940. Rebuilt in 1947, it was destroyed by fire again in 1959.[12]

Before the fish-reduction plant there had been a small industry using a fine stand of cedar behind Shingle Bay. The first roofing shakes cut there were shipped to Victoria on Captain Henry Paxton's sealing schooner, the *Wanderer*. Later the Harris brothers, Howard and Stanley, who had given up on farming, brought in a portable sawmill to cut lumber and shingles. They also acquired the first powerboat on the island in 1902, the 30-foot steam launch *Pearl*, which they used in a trading business among the islands. Howard Harris married Clara Menzies in 1906 and moved the sawmill to Hope Bay, where he also built boats.

In the 1920s the Japanese established a herring saltery and fish-processing plant at Otter Bay, where their fishing fleet was based. Seiners operated in Swanson Channel. The herring was packed in

400-pound boxes for export to China and Japan; when the boxes arrived the surplus salt was scraped off and sold.

In earlier years the Japanese cut cordwood fuel for the Fraser River cannery steam plants on property owned by a Mr. Hiashi between Otter Bay and James Point. Others made charcoal in pits as on Mayne for export, but the Japanese did not purchase farm land on Pender. Most of them worked as labourers for white settlers.

SOUTH PENDER ISLAND

Meanwhile, on South Pender, 23-year-old Arthur Reed Spalding had begun in 1886 with 800 acres from the old Tod-Alexander property. Spalding had left Ore Place in England in 1884 seeking adventure and had spent time in New Orleans, California, and Oregon before landing in Victoria. He was taken to Bedwell Harbour from Sidney by his friend David Ker of the pioneer Saanich milling firm of Brackman and Ker.

Spalding later pre-empted additional land, including some on

Front, l. to r. Agnes McKay, Lilias Spalding. Back, l. to r. Charles Lowe, Gerry Payne, Arthur Spalding, Arthur Lowe. (COURTESY BC ARCHIVES.)

North Pender. He had started in partnership with Charles Long, a boyhood friend from Sussex, but Long subsequently teamed up with Gerald F. Richardson of Bedwell Harbour. Long and Richardson once made a quixotic attempt to drive a small herd of sheep into the Klondike. Like many another ill-conceived foray into the north, this one was a failure. Long did better on Pender raising birds for Sunday-morning cock-fights. He gave up on the west coast in 1901, however, and returned to England.

Samuel Beddis came over from Salt Spring to build a five-bedroom house for Arthur and his wife Lilias at Little Bay, looking across Plumper Sound to Saturna. The lumber was dragged across the island from Bedwell Harbour by oxen.

Arthur sailed nine miles to Beddis's place at Beaver Point once a month for mail. On one of these trips he capsized in a storm. A mailbag was lost, but Spalding made it safely to shore. After that misadventure, the mail was switched to Mayne, where it was relayed to South Pender via Saturna by Spalding, Harold Payne or Constable Drummond.

Spalding was the official South Pender postmaster initially, but his wife handled the office work and took over in 1900 when the steamship *Iroquois* went into service. Her first post office was a lean-to against the freight shed on the Bedwell Harbour wharf. Lilias often waited up until after midnight for the mail to arrive. She held the position until her death at 81 in 1951. Arthur had died at 69 in 1932. By 1966 there were five generations of Spalding and seven generations of McKay (Lilias's family) descendants living on Pender.

Lilias Spalding's son-in-law, John Freeman, who succeeded her as postmaster, used an automobile to deliver mail and persuaded residents to put signals on their mailboxes. The Herbert Spaldings put up a handsomely crafted cedar-bark box with a slanting roof to which they hung the shredded remains of lace-trimmed blue nylon panties if mail was to be picked up. The Craddocks used white rags; Mrs. Cathy McDonald a red and white bandana. Freeman complained that Mrs. Ruby Hatcher's mailbox was full of earwigs and the Huttons' had wasps. Constance Grey put up a beachcombed red and green fishing flag at her cottage, "Clakili."[13]

There was an Indian fishing settlement on Hay Point at the entrance to Bedwell Harbour in the 1880s, but the East Saanich tribe caused little trouble for the newcomers. There were about 80 Indians during the summer months and half of them stayed over the winter in permanent dwellings. "They were wonderful neighbours," Spalding's daughter Beatrice later recalled. "I remember my father used to tell me that when there was nobody else about he'd go off perhaps in the boat for a week or a month and he'd just go and tell the Indians he'd be away and to keep an eye on things. Nothing was ever taken."[14]

Alex Hamilton's daughter Mary reinforced this view: "We didn't have any feeling that we were replacing those people," she said, "or that we were displacing them. I don't know why. But they must have felt, you know, that that place belonged to them because they had known it long before we were there, but they didn't make any protests as long as we were around."[15]

The Spaldings also had a number of Japanese working for them, on the land and in the house. "Everyone in those days had Jap boys," Constance Grey later recalled. This generalization applied to only the few moneyed families on the islands, however.[16]

Having help around the place allowed these families to take life easier than most of their neighbours on the other islands. The men took time off for hunting expeditions and trips to Victoria. Some maintained rooms in the capital; others, like Warburton Pike, stayed at the Union Club. Beatrice Spalding recalled that her father took the family camping for two weeks each summer to such spots as Saanich Inlet, Goldstream, and the Malahat.

Arthur Spalding was a cultured man who read voraciously, wrote poetry and sketched. His family had been involved in the publishing business as well as owning a number of paper mills in England. Spalding had brought a number of books from his family home and sent for others after his arrival on Pender. In time he built up a library of 2,000 volumes. In 1899 Arthur wrote to his wife that a six-volume set of Edward Gibbon's *Decline and Fall of the Roman Empire* had just arrived from England.

Lilias acted as den-mother to the roving bachelors of South Pender and Saturna, and the Spalding house was a gathering place.

Arthur Spalding. (COURTESY BC ARCHIVES)

Strangers were always arriving and staying for a meal or a bed overnight. Most of the South Pender residents visited there on Christmas Day.

It was not all fun and games, however. Arthur and his wife were hard workers. They tilled the land with oxen and grew wheat for the chickens. Arthur made frequent two-day trips to Nanaimo in his sloop to take his sheep to market, where prices were better because of the coal mines. Lilias was a good shot and brought down numerous deer. There were also four children to raise: a son Herbert, and daughters Helen, Elizabeth and Beatrice. Herbert later married Winifred Bellhouse of Galiano.

Lilias Spalding baked bread and buns, and made butter and cottage cheese. "Every day there were lamps to fill, wicks to trim, and chimneys to polish. When the grapes were ripe, she made gallons of rosé wine. She made pickles, jams and jellies, bottles and bottles of preserves, and she even bottled venison, grouse, and salmon. When a pig was slaughtered she rendered the lard and cured her own hams and bacon, and most afternoons she found time to work at her loom."[17]

Settlement on South Pender expanded steadily during the 1890s. After his year on Saturna, Leonard Higgs and his wife Emma had bought property alongside "Uncle Arthur" and built a home they called "Kloshe Illahee," a Chinook phrase meaning "good land." Higgs, like many of his young countrymen, got caught up in the Klondike gold fever but returned empty-handed from three summers in the north, so he turned his hand to ranching on Pender and taking a variety of jobs available nearby, such as logging and working on fixed trap-nets for catching salmon.

In 1894 Higgs sold a piece of his property to Arthur E. Stanford, who had moved to the island with his partner Elijah Pollard after giving the Cariboo gold rush a try. Stanford, who called his ranch "Southlands," rowed to Friday Harbor on San Juan Island to buy cheaper groceries. He often neglected to report his purchases, a practice which is said to still exist among some Bedwell boaters today.

Pollard pre-empted land at Tilly Point, where Stanford helped him build a house. The two men also worked together raising a barn and haying. Pollard was road foreman in 1908 and later moved to North Pender.

One of the first industries was the cutting of props for shoring up mine tunnels. In the early 1890s four big sea-going schooners loaded up in Bedwell Harbour with the little logs for Mexico and South America. The props were of varying lengths, not more than ten inches at the butt and four inches at the top.

Bigger logs were hauled out on skid roads by oxen to a camp at Wallace Point, on the southern tip of North Pender at the entrance to Bedwell Harbour. A number of new houses were built by carpenters who came from Victoria with their materials loaded on scows. They worked from dawn until dark without a day's rest until the house was finished, sometimes in as little as two weeks.

There was still no wharf on South Pender by 1896 and residents rowed three miles across to Saturna to pick up supplies from the steamers. On more than one occasion oxen were pushed into the water from the *R.P. Rithet* and *Iroquois* in Bedwell Harbour to swim ashore. The nearest doctor was at Ganges, and since there was no telephone a boat had to be sent to fetch him.

The construction of a wharf in Bedwell Harbour at the turn of the century facilitated the first regular steamship service to South Pender. The stubby little *Iroquois* started the run in 1901. The island's one-room school was on the bluff above the wharf and the children joined the parade to the pier on boat-days. Arthur Spalding's ox team was tied to a big yew on the hill and was the subject of many photographs by tourists during stopovers.

In 1905 Captain John F. Parry of H.M.S. *Egeria*, carrying out tidal survey work in the area, supervised construction of a cabin on the shore of Bedwell Harbour to house one or two of his men who were recording the tides. The skipper was also prevailed upon in that year by Gilbert Ainslie to lend men to dismantle his log house on Saturna and move it to the north shore of South Pender to re-erect. Ainslie's Pender property was later taken over by the adventurer Ernest G. Beaumont ("Captain Beaumont"), who gave 500 acres to the government for a park named in his honour.

The rural character and appearance of South Pender have changed little over the past century. There were only five households at the turn of the century and the resident population is still only about 125, but proposed new developments on Bedwell Harbour could result in dramatic changes. The population of North Pender jumped to 1,400 with the Magic Lakes subdivision, but the island has still been able to retain much of the charm that attracted the early settlers, most of whom came from the British Isles.

Smugglers, Millionaires
and Lepers

Before the boundary dispute between the U.S. and Britain was settled in 1872, islanders moved freely back and forth between the San Juan and the Gulf Islands. When the Emperor of Germany, acting as an arbitrator, decreed that the border should pursue a zigzag route between the islands, some settlers didn't see why they should change their ways. Pender and Saturna residents sailed over to Friday Harbor to buy cheaper groceries, and so the smuggling era was born. It began with groceries and wool, then moved up to opium and Chinese immigrants, and rum-running in the days of American prohibition.

The business naturally flourished on those islands nearest the boundary line—Saturna and South Pender on the Canadian side, and San Juan and Orcas on the American, and a number of smaller islands on both sides. Many of the transactions occurred in Boundary Pass, off East Point and Patos Island lighthouses at one end, and

Turn Point lighthouse on Stuart Island on the American side at the other.

At the time of the border settlement, the price of opium was $45 a can in the U.S. and $15 in Canada, which made it a profitable item for smugglers. Opium was more easily obtained in B.C. to supply the large number of Chinese residents who had been brought in as labourers. Much of the opium came in on the Empress liners from the Orient. Bags would be dropped off the stern to be picked up by waiting launches. Len Bittancourt of Salt Spring worked for Canada Customs which attempted to follow the ships from the William Head Quarantine Station across the strait into Vancouver. The Empresses travelled at 18 knots in some stretches of water and it was difficult to keep up. When they did get aboard, the Customs men often had to shovel through coal looking for hidden opium. Bittancourt was on his father's boat, the *Winnemac*, when it was chartered by the government for such work before Customs had its own vessels. [1]

American law was restrictive on Oriental immigration, and smugglers charged individuals $50 to take them across the line into the U.S. On some occasions, when the smugglers feared interception, they simply dropped the unwitting Chinese back on the Canadian shore in the dark of night and told them it was the U.S.

The price differential for wool was almost the same as for opium: five dollars per hundredweight in Canada and ten dollars in the U.S. That was too much of a temptation for some Gulf Island sheep ranchers, who found it more profitable to sell wool to the Americans. Rustlers in the San Juans stepped up their activity, raiding Gulf Island farms and taking back wool on the hoof.

The most notable of the wool smugglers was diminutive Alfred Burke of little Shaw Island in the San Juans. Burke had a long, slender rowboat stained a dull black, "the colour of sea water," for camouflage. He started across the channel near the end of the flood tide, keeping a wary eye out for Constable Arthur Drummond. Only his hat would be visible above the gunwales.

"During each year's shearing season he would quietly ride the changing tide across Haro Strait to the Gulf Islands—appearing, then, at one sheep ranch after another, offering to trade chickens,

77

tobacco or cash for fleeces. In his long black coat and slouch hat the grey-bearded Burke became a familiar figure to Canadian islanders, one of whom recalled that he rowed standing up, without feathering his oars, for fear the sun would reflect from the wet blades."[2]

The settlers kept the transactions as circumspect as possible. They would carefully leave a roll of fleeces in their barns for Burke to pick up quietly and leave the agreed-upon payment in money or groceries and candies for the children. (Eggs were five cents a dozen cheaper in the San Juans.) Most settlers regarded Burke simply as a nice little man.

Burke, in fact, was only a middleman. On returning with his illicit cargo to the San Juans he had to sell the wool to various sheep ranchers on different islands. All went well until one rancher on San Juan Island with only 100 sheep shipped 30 tons of wool, almost all of which he had bought from Burke, to the market at Port Townsend. Suspicions were aroused and the Revenue inspectors began sniffing about. What they discovered was that more wool was being shipped through Seattle and Port Townsend "than could possibly grow on the backs of all the sheep on the whole Rosario Archipelago and Customs returns showed little or no evidence of importation."[3]

It didn't take the agents long to get on Burke's trail. They simply went over to Pender and Saturna and surreptitiously marked some bundles of wool in the barns by inserting little wooden pegs. When the wool showed up in a storekeeper's warehouse on Orcas Island, Burke was arrested at his home. Many islanders were relieved when he was later acquitted at a trial in Friday Harbor. The judge ruled that the agents had not actually seen Burke cross the boundary with the contraband wool.

Another man who conducted a busy trade across Boundary Pass was Victor McConnell, the son of a pioneer family who lived not far from Burke on little McConnell Island in the San Juans. "McConnell is said never to have crossed the border empty: hauled everything from apples to shoes to the Canadian side, in exchange for sugar and other staples 'imported' on the return trip." The sugar, cheaper on the Canadian side, was sold to an Orcas storekeeper who dumped it out of the British-brand sacks and sold it in bulk.[4]

It was one thing for harmless little men such as Burke and McConnell to be carrying on a "free trade" business in wool and groceries, but in the Prohibition era the smuggling stakes became much higher. More capital was required to buy liquor, and large, speedy vessels to move it across the border into the thirsty U.S. Sea routes were the favoured way of transport, and secluded coves in the Gulf Islands became rendezvous points. Transfers were made there from launches to smaller "runners" of gunny-sacks containing a dozen bottles. The sacks were easier to handle than cardboard or wooden cases and if it was necessary to toss them hurriedly overboard they could eventually be recovered, because it took a long time for burlap sacks to disintegrate in saltwater. One sack-maker in Victoria was said to have sold 3,000 bags a week to just one of his customers at the height of the smuggling boom.

Some islanders became involved in the business for a time, being paid by the rum-runners to allow liquor to be stashed for a few days in their woodsheds and barns for pickup men. Robert Roe told one of them, "I don't care what you're doing as long as you don't go stealing any of our sheep." At first it was regarded in the same light as wool smuggling, but it soon grew apparent that this was more serious. The stakes grew so high that it was not long before hardened criminals moved in. When hi-jackings and violence became common, the settlers opted out.[5]

More drops and transfers began to be made at sea, or in secluded bays or on uninhabited islets. D'Arcy Island became a favourite spot to make caches because few Customs men wanted to go poking around the leper colony.

MORESBY ISLAND

Each of the smaller settled islands nestled between the major Gulf Islands has a history of its own. None is more colourful than that of Moresby. This 1,600-acre island lying only three miles northeast of the Swartz Bay ferry terminal has been occupied since 1863.

One of the early settlers was W.A. Hollins, of whom little is known except that he grew plums on a patch of land he cleared on his 1,100 acres, starting in 1869. The trees bore fruit for more than

Horatio Robertson. (COURTESY BC ARCHIVES)

a century and Moresby was often referred to as "Plum Island." Hollins held on until 1888, when he sold to Captain Horatio John "Race" Robertson.

Robertson had just moved to B.C. after 35 years in China, where he had been a tea clipper seaman, pilot on the Yangtze River and merchant in his birthplace of Foochow. His father had been named Horatio by *his* father, who had been a signal officer under Admiral Horatio Nelson. The hero's name had been passed along to the next generation. Robertson's wife was the daughter of a wealthy British trader in China; the couple had three daughters and eight sons. The family left China because the climate was beginning to wear on them, and Robertson wanted to set up a tea-importing business in Canada. He was also involved for a short time in the shipping and whaling industries in B.C.

It was with his large family in mind that Robertson set to work designing a house on his new property on Moresby. He laid out two octagonal towers joined by a 100-foot verandah which was later glassed in. One of the towers was for the boys; the other for Robertson, his wife, and the three girls, as well as a dining-room and kitchen. The family got together for meals served by a Chinese couple they had brought with them from Foochow. The walls of the three-storey towers were built of ten-inch-thick timbers coated with plaster on the outside, the first seen in B.C. The walls were meant to withstand Indian bullets, which Robertson had no doubt heard tales of in China.

After buying out Hollins, Robertson acquired the remainder of the island from the government. He had 60 acres under cultivation but was not a success as a farmer. When he tried to involve his sons in the work, they rebelled. Some ran off to sea, others were sent to schools in Europe.

Attempting to bring over Chinese labourers, Robertson became embroiled in a dispute with Canadian government officials over the "head tax" on importing Chinese indentured labour. When some Indians he had hired for farm work failed to show up, Robertson is said to have set fire to their village, in the manner of the Royal Navy at the time. He was ordered to pay compensation in this instance, however, since the punishment didn't fit the offence.

Antics like this soon gave Robertson the reputation of a mean-spirited man, hot-tempered and hard on his workers. He had spent too many years as an overseer in China. Victorians were bemused to see him on occasion being pulled in a rickshaw along city streets by

Agnes (Mrs. Horatio) Robertson. (COURTESY BC ARCHIVES)

one of his coolies. Robertson was constantly launching lawsuits, which he invariably lost.

His notoriety peaked in February 1889, when the Chinese couple attempted to escape from their Moresby servitude. When the Robertsons threatened to separate the pair by sending the man back to China, they decided to make a break for freedom. After putting together a crude raft with three logs and a board lashed with ropes, the couple pushed off. They hoped to reach Beaver Point to the north on Salt Spring, but the tide and a cold north wind laced with sleet drove them southward down Haro Strait. They had no food or water, only a trunk containing their possessions.

The pair drifted for two nights and three days before being spotted. An Indian fisherman in a canoe saw them bobbing in the waves off Cadboro Bay. Both were stiff with cold and barely conscious. When word of their rescue and mistreatment on the island reached the *Colonist*, the newspaper carried a front-page story with lurid details of life with the Robertsons.

Robertson marched to his lawyer once again and launched a $25,000 libel suit against the newspaper. The case went to trial in June before Judge Henry Crease. It went on for days, with both the *Colonist* and the *Standard* playing up the most sensational testimony. At one point Robertson claimed the man was going to be sent home because he had intended to put his wife into prostitution in Victoria. Robertson also pleaded that he had property in China which his sons were to inherit, and the Chinese government might retaliate against him because of the unfavourable news story.

On the other hand, Robertson admitted he owed the couple money in wages which had been withheld. The woman said Mrs. Robertson had smacked her, while the man complained the Robertson boys were cruel to him. After all the evidence had been heard, Judge Crease ruled that although there was libel, Robertson's reputation had not been injured and there should be no damages. It was generally regarded as a wise verdict, since Robertson's reputation had not been good even before the case.

Robertson eventually gave up on Moresby and moved to Victoria, where he became interested in politics. His arrogance repelled any supporters he might have had, however, and he settled for writing cranky letters to the editor. He died in 1903, aged 69. The family squabbled over the estate and the island was purchased by Thomas W. Paterson in 1906.

Three years later Paterson was named Lieutenant-Governor and soon took advantage of his revived political clout to get a wharf on Moresby built by the government for his private use. He regarded the island primarily as a bird-hunting preserve. Paterson was interested in having the farm developed, however, and leased it to a white-bearded Quaker, Stanley Harris, who had settled at Shingle Bay on Pender with his brother Howard.

Harris, who had studied agriculture in Ontario, soon developed a profitable farm on Moresby, primarily with prize Jersey cattle. Paterson helped finance the purchase of livestock and machinery. As well as cattle, Harris raised pigs, sheep and turkeys. The produce was picked up and taken to the railhead at Sidney by Paterson's steamship, the *Iroquois*. In 1915 Harris married Ella Ruckle of Salt Spring Island. He wore a white shirt, high stiff collar and tie all day, every day. He was able to stay clean by working mostly with his poultry and bees. Japanese labourers mucked out the barns and did other dirty work. Harris also ran a gasoline launch to carry cans of milk and cream to Sidney to be transported by train to Victoria.

Paterson died in 1921 and three years later his widow sold the island to a wealthy American mine-owner, Lewis Bradbury, and Harris left. An eccentric bachelor who spent only short summer periods on the island, Bradbury went broke in 1933 and lost title to Moresby. The island had a number of owners, some of them absentees, in succeeding years as its value escalated. In 1960 it was bought by a German syndicate for $170,000. Fifteen years later the island was sold for $2.9 million.

PIERS ISLAND

Piers, the 240-acre island directly across from the Swartz Bay ferry terminal, was first owned by Clive Phillipps-Wolley around the turn of the century. Phillipps-Wolley was a direct descendant of Robert Clive, who had amassed a fortune while conquering India for the British Empire.

Phillipps-Wolley had first visited Victoria in 1884 at the end of a North American hunting expedition. He liked what he saw so much that he left England in 1890 with his wife Jane and four children for Victoria, where he built a large house for his family on 16 acres of prime land in Oak Bay. Phillipps-Wolley wrote poetry in the Kipling style and articles on B.C. for British journals, as well as vigorous western romance tales which were said to have persuaded young men in England to emigrate to western Canada.[6]

An adventuring friend and business partner of Warburton Pike, Phillipps-Wolley tired of life in Oak Bay after about ten years and moved to Piers, where he built another home. But life soon paled there, too, and the family moved on in 1908 to the Duncan area. He died there in 1918 after being knighted for his work in founding the B.C. Navy League and writing the 1911 Coronation hymn for King George V. Sir Clive remained an ardent Conservative and imperialist to the end.

The Piers property was bought in 1908 by Lieutenant-Colonel J.S. Harvey of Victoria, a grandson of Robert Dunsmuir. Harvey lived on the island for only four years before selling it for $60,000 to an English syndicate which planned to build a three-storey, 32-room resort hotel. The project went ahead as planned but the building burned down shortly before completion. There had been bitter labour problems during construction; arson was suspected but never proven. Because the syndicate was then unable to complete its payments, the island reverted to Harvey and stayed in his family for the next 45 years.

It passed into the hands of a son, lawyer Robert Harvey of Victoria, who leased it to sheep grazers for 20 years. In 1932 the federal government expropriated Piers to use it as a detention camp for the troublesome Sons of Freedom Doukhobor sect. A total of $350,000 was spent to erect separate barracks for 295 men and 280 women. In its bureaucratic naivety, the government had thought it could keep the men and women separated by putting a 14-foot barbed wire barrier between the barracks. Needless to say, the prisoners came up with a variety of means of scaling the fence and getting together to flout the rules. An added problem was the chanting of the Doukhobors, which bothered the owners of nearby Knapp

Island. The camp was disbanded in 1934 and the Freedomites released.

During the war Piers was used by the armed services for amphibious assault training. Bob Harvey later got the island back and had it listed for sale for many years without any takers. Eventually it was bought by developers who introduced a unique subdivision plan with waterfront lots and a common-owned central park.

PORTLAND ISLAND

During the 1840s and '50s the Hudson's Bay Company brought in as many as 400 Hawaiians to work on its timber holdings and farms on Puget Sound and San Juan Island. They also acted as interpreters for the fur traders, having a facility with the languages of the various tribes which the whites, who conversed with the natives only in the Chinook jargon, were unable to acquire. When their contracts with the company expired, a number of these people, known as "Kanakas," decided to settle rather than return home. Some went first in 1859 to 480-acre Portland Island, just west of Moresby, which had been given to them by the H.B.C. Other Hawaiians, seamen on the trans-Pacific run, are said to have jumped ship while passing near the islands.

The leader of the Kanakas was William Naukana, a cousin of King Kamehameha IV, who had been born on Maui in 1813 and came to work for the company at Fort Vancouver in 1840, later settling on San Juan Island. After San Juan was ceded to the U.S. by the boundary arbitration commission in 1872, Naukana returned to the Sandwich Islands, as they were then known, for a visit, and brought 17 more of his people to settle on Isabella Point on Salt Spring and the adjacent Isabella islets. Many of the Hawaiians married Indian women and built log houses. They grew tobacco and cured it with imported molasses and rum.

Naukana later sold Portland Island to Clive Phillipps-Wolley, and in 1928, it came into the hands of the swashbuckling Frank A. "One-Armed" Sutton. Born in England in 1884, Sutton had lost an arm in the First World War at Gallipoli. Despite the wound, he went next to China as a soldier of fortune. He loved to gamble and won a fortune betting on horse races there. Sutton turned up next in B.C. where he bought Portland Island with the intention of raising horses. He built a 40-horse stable and planted plum and apple trees; he also kept pens stocked with pheasants for hunting. The end of these luxury days came suddenly in 1929 when the stock-market crash wiped out Sutton's fortune. The mortgage on the island was foreclosed and Sutton went back to China, where he worked for a time as a war correspondent for the Hearst newspaper chain.

Salt Spring entrepreneur Gavin Mouat became the next owner of Portland Island about 1932. In 1957 he swapped it to the provincial government for some timber elsewhere. The island was then "given" to Princess Margaret during a visit she made to B.C. in 1958, renamed in her honour, and turned into a marine park in 1967.

JAMES ISLAND

The first settlers on 780-acre James Island off the Saanich Peninsula arrived in the 1870s. A few farmers owned land until the 1890s, when ownership of the entire island was acquired by "The James Island Club," made up of prominent Victorians, including future premier Richard McBride. The club turned the island into a private hunting reserve. A lodge was built and partridge, quail, grouse and pheasants and other game, including mountain sheep, were introduced, although the sandy, rock-less island has no hills. It is wooded, however, with fir, cedar and arbutus.

Around the turn of the century ownership of the island passed into the hands of Dr. G.L. and Lady Sybil Findlay. In 1907 the Findlays sold it to George Wheatcroft, a wealthy English railroader, who intended to turn it into a private park. Wheatcroft imported fallow deer from the estate of the Duke of Devonshire. In 1913 Wheatcroft sold the island to Canadian Explosives Ltd. as a site for manufacturing dynamite.

In 1915 a thousand construction workers were employed on the island to rush into operation a plant to meet the war-time demand for explosives. They lived in a tent village and hastily constructed bunkhouses. The plant became the first in Canada to manufacture the newly invented T.N.T., more powerful than dynamite, for war-time weapons. Five hundred men worked at the plant and produced a total of 35,000,000 pounds of T.N.T. by the end of the war in 1918.

Production of T.N.T. and dynamite continued after the war on a smaller scale with 100 employees in the 1920s. Many were Chinese, who lived in the bunkhouses. Other staff lived in company-built houses on the island or commuted daily from the Sidney area on a 29-passenger ferry. The plant operation was cut back in 1962 and the little settlement closed down. A small number of workers continued to commute until the plant was closed and the island sold in 1978 by Canadian Industries Ltd., which succeeded C.E.L. It is now slated for residential development.

SIDNEY ISLAND

In 1860 the H.B.C. surveyed Sidney Island into lots for auction, with an upset price of six shillings an acre, but the sale was abandoned for lack of interest. Prospective buyers were said to be fearful of attacks by Indians. The island then fell somehow into the hands of George Hunter Cary, who served a controversial term as attorney-general in the Colonial government under Governor James Douglas. After Cary was ousted and returned to England, the island lay more or less dormant until 1902, except for a 15-acre farm operated by Chinese at the south end. In that year George L. Courtney, freight and passenger agent for the C.P.R. in Victoria, bought it for $25,000.

Courtney imported pheasants from China and organized shooting parties. After finding a large clay deposit at the north end, he established the Sidney Island Brick and Tile Company in 1906. The plant produced 55,000 bricks a year for the next three years; some went into the building of the Empress Hotel, the Hotel Vancouver and the C.P.R. depot in Vancouver, and some were shipped north to the new mining town of Anyox. The brickyard employed 70 men, most of them Chinese.

The brickyard struggled, however, and in 1909 Courtney sold the island to pay off his debts. The buyers were ten Victoria businessmen who formed a syndicate with $15,000 each for the purchase price of $150,000. Courtney retained 200 choice acres containing the brickyard at the north end, but lost them after going bankrupt during the war. The government acquired his property and turned it into the Sidney Spit Marine Park.

The syndicate included cement-maker R.P. Butchart, the W. & J. Wilson clothing family and Ernest Todd of the salmon-canning Todd family. Between 1943 and 1961 the Todds purchased another eight shares to gain control of the island and prevent a sale to California interests. One-tenth of the island remained in the hands of R.B. Wilson. The island was sold again in the 1970s to a new syndicate, despite requests to the government to buy it for a park. The future of the island, which has almost 15 miles of sandy beaches, is uncertain.

D'ARCY ISLAND

D'Arcy Island was owned briefly by J.H. Garrett in 1886. Six years later it was taken over by the federal government to be used as a leper colony, a function it served for the next 32 years. Beginning

The leper colony on D'Arcy Island. (COURTESY BC ARCHIVES)

with just one lonely victim, the island was later a place of exile for half a dozen people at a time. They lived in horrible conditions in little huts, supplied with food, clothing and a ration of opium four times a year. Attempts to escape often ended in death by drowning. In 1924 the lepers were moved to tiny Bentinck Island, off the southern tip of Vancouver Island between Race Rocks and Rocky Point and close to the quarantine station. The colony remained there, with as many as 20 leprosy victims at one time, until the last one died in 1956. This island is now a provincial marine park.

PREVOST ISLAND

Prevost Island was bought by Digby Hussey de Burgh in 1924. He raised sheep, goats and cattle, with 130 acres of seed pasture and 1,000 acres of rough pasture. He had left Ireland at the age of 19 and farmed in Manitoba and Alberta before moving out in 1892 to Beaver Point on Salt Spring, where he lived for several years. After a stint back in Ireland farming the family estate in County Limerick, de Burgh returned to B.C. and acquired Prevost. In 1938 he went into business in Vancouver and died there at 80 in 1951. His sons Hubert and Harlowen retained the island property and most of it has stayed in the family's hands.

Aussies, Blacks
and the Squire

A t 120 square miles, Salt Spring is the largest of the southern
Gulf Islands. Its proximity to the Saanich Peninsula at the south
end and the Cowichan district to the west contributed to the island's
early development.

Returning from the 1858 Fraser River gold rush after failing to
strike it rich, a number of men began looking for land on which to
settle. Most of the prime property around Victoria had been taken
up by Hudson's Bay Company officers, and adjacent property was
too expensive for the goldhunters who had lost their savings in a bid
for quick riches. The price of land was five dollars an acre, with a
down payment of one-quarter of the total price. The balance was to
be paid over the next four years at five percent interest. Failure to
pay resulted in the property reverting to the Crown without compensation for improvements. Land in Washington Territory was
much cheaper, but Governor Douglas rejected pleas for change.

In the spring of 1859 a group of penniless Australian land-seekers approached Victoria lawyer John Copland for help. He agreed, knowing that the bush-wise men from down under would make good homesteaders. Copland was an aggressive Scotsman who had spent six years in Australia before being lured to Victoria by the gold rush with a number of Aussies, many of whom now had no funds to return home or move elsewhere. Copland soon became active in Victoria's raucous politics, allying himself with the anti-establishment newspaper editor Amor De Cosmos in opposition to Douglas's autocratic rule. It was not surprising, then, that Douglas rejected the Copland group's petition to be allowed to settle in the Cowichan River valley. Instead, Douglas offered unsurveyed land in the Chemainus area, including part of Salt Spring Island, for a pre-emption fee of a shilling an acre, with no payment until surveys had been completed. Pre-emption for speculative purposes was discouraged by the requirements to make improvements on the land.

On July 18, 1859, a group of 29 potential settlers, now expanded to include a few English, Scots, Irish and Blacks, set off on the steamer *Nanaimo Packet* to investigate Chemainus, but their interest was caught *en route* as the vessel passed Salt Spring. When the group returned, Copland went to the Land Office and was offered better terms than Chemainus: the 29 prospective settlers could pre-empt on the island and pay only after a survey was completed by the Colonial government of Vancouver Island.

On July 27 the first group of 17 arrived to begin choosing sites. Some of them had enough money to buy basic equipment. "Others had nothing apart from an axe, an adze, a hammer and a bag of nails, bag of flour, iron cook pot, much enthusiasm, grit and determination."[1]

The 17 included Armstead Buckner, one of about 600 Blacks who had come to Victoria from San Francisco at the time of the Fraser gold rush with the encouragement of Governor Douglas. Contrary to popular opinion, few were runaway slaves. Some came from the Caribbean and others had bought or were granted their freedom from slavery before moving to California. A few had become successful businessmen in San Francisco, but were discouraged by growing anti-Black sentiment and restrictive laws in California.

More than a dozen Blacks came to Salt Spring soon after Buckner, who had settled south of St. Mary Lake on the site of the present-day golf course. It is another common misconception that they formed a "colony" on the island. Douglas encouraged them to settle, but as individuals rather than a group. In fact the Blacks often squabbled among themselves and a few "violent hatreds" sprang up.[2]

After Buckner, other Blacks who came to the island in the fall of 1859 included William Robinson, brothers John C., Elias and William Jones, William Isaacs, Levi Davis, Daniel Fredison, Hiram Whims, Abraham Copeland and his son-in-law, W.L. Harrison, and Fielding Spotts.

Spotts, a cooper by trade, farmed for a number of years at the north end, but left with his family in the 1870s to settle on the Saanich peninsula. There he became a school trustee and his nine children were active in sports. Discouraged by Indian violence and various difficulties, a number of other Blacks left about the same time and only ten families remained in 1875, although their numbers increased later.

Once on the island the Blacks dispersed to different districts, although the majority at first were around Ganges Harbour. Over the years there was considerable intermarriage among whites, Indians, Hawaiians and Blacks, creating a unique Gulf Islands racial mix. Racial prejudice was absent to a remarkable degree on Salt Spring, and the Blacks were accepted by most from the start, in contrast to their experience in Victoria. Like the white settlers, the Blacks had trouble with the Indians during the first decade on the island. Although the Cowichan Indians who frequented the island did not maintain permanent residence there, they resented the sudden intrusion of settlers on what they had always considered to be their land.

For centuries the Indians had come to the island to dig clams, hunt ducks, gather berries and fish for herring and salmon. They also collected camas bulbs to pound into flour, as well as mushrooms, medicinal herbs and cascara bark. Even after white settlement, as many as 500 Indians and a few Hawaiians gathered in Ganges Harbour on May and June low-tide nights for clamming. They filled five-gallon coal-oil tins with pitch to set afire for light. Others congregated in Fulford Harbour to hunt ducks. Up to two dozen canoes would be strung out across the harbour, flushing up birds to be brought down by bow and arrow and, later, with muzzle-loaded shotguns.[3]

There is evidence that the attacks on settlers, and, more commonly, the theft of animals and crops, were perpetrated by a relatively small number of individual Indians who clashed repeatedly with the law. The majority of the Cowichans got on well with the settlers, who allowed them to continue picking berries and hunting on their properties.

Among the first group of 17 settlers were Thomas Henry Lineker, his wife, the widow of an Australian sea captain when she married Lineker, and her daughter. Mrs. Lineker was the first white woman on the island. With the aid of the others they built a house in the summer of 1859 at the head of Ganges Harbour, near the site of the present Harbour House Hotel. Later in the year their child was the first born to Salt Spring settlers.

Mrs. Lineker was one of the few whites on the island who did not accept the Black settlers on terms of equality. Explaining that she had been brought up as "the daughter of a Church of England clergyman," Mrs. Lineker said she could not mix with them and refused to meet or worship in the same room.[4]

A student of the classics at Rugby School under Matthew Arnold, Tom Lineker was one of the most intelligent and level-headed of the new arrivals. He was also one of the few to own a rifle. This weapon was to play a part in the first major incident of violence on Salt Spring, in the summer of 1860. A number of varying accounts of the incident have been written, but Lineker's is regarded as the most reliable.

On July 4 a party of 14 Bella Bella Indians from the north coast and a renegade white trader identified as John McCawley stopped over in Ganges Harbour in a big canoe bound for Victoria with a load of furs. About 50 Cowichans were already camped at the head of the harbour. Long-standing hostility between the two tribes erupted and the Cowichans killed eight Bella Bella men.

During the melee McCawley slipped off to Lineker's house nearby. Fearing the Indians might continue their rampage, Lineker sent his wife and two children off into the bush to hide while he returned to the beach to survey the carnage. When he went back to the house McCawley had disappeared, with Lineker's gun. Lineker speculated that McCawley was in league with the Cowichans, with whom he had worked in the past, and that he later sold the northerners' furs in Victoria.

McCawley was an Englishman who came to Vancouver Island via Hawaii, San Francisco and New Westminster. He was said to have fled Hawaii to avoid embezzlement charges, and had left San Francisco in a similar hurry. In New Westminster he had been charged with assault but was acquitted. McCawley was described as "a ladies' man," tall, slim, blue-eyed and handsome with a carefully curled and waxed moustache.

There is speculation that "McCawley" might be the same person as the "Macaulay" identified by Captain J.T. Walbran as the man responsible for setting off the 1858 gold rush to the Fraser River. In 1857, while the U.S. survey vessel *Active* was in Semiahmoo Bay fixing the 49th-parallel boundary line with H.M.S. *Plumper*, a man called Macaulay was arrested by ship's officers for selling liquor in the surveying camps. On the way to Esquimalt to face the charge, Macaulay "showed the crew of the *Active* a large quantity of gold dust which he had received in trade from the Fraser River Indians. The crew on arrival at San Francisco the following winter spread the news, and the rush to the Fraser of 1858 was the result."[5]

Lineker wrote Douglas after the Indian battle on Salt Spring, seeking more protection for the islanders, but when the governor took no action, the settlers joined together to save their crops and animals from marauders. A number of American outlaws based in the San Juans sold guns to the Indians and teamed up with them in raids on homesteads. Salt Spring's indented shoreline made their work easy: plunderers could slip in and out of the bays and harbours undetected. During the 1860s roving Cowichans would shoot randomly at lighted Salt Spring cabins on the shoreline during the night.

Despite such incidents, settlement continued. By the end of August 1859, almost all of the original group of 29 land-seekers had taken up property and another 32 had applied through Copland. In December there were 56 new applicants and Salt Spring was on its way to becoming the most populated of the Gulf Islands. By the end of the year there were more than 70 settlers, of whom 53 were Australians. Many of the Aussies were illiterate, but they proved to be resourceful handymen—optimistic, friendly and co-operative as well as self-reliant. They made ideal pioneers on the rough brush- and forest-covered island.

The first industry on Salt Spring was a sandstone quarry at Vesuvius Bay, which started operations in 1860. In that year flagstones were cut for Victoria's first sidewalks. In later years Vesuvius sandstone went into the building of the Esquimalt Graving Dock and was exported to San Francisco for a new federal mint.

Among the first white settlers in 1859 were John Patton Booth, a native of the Orkney Islands who was only 21 when he arrived, and Henry Sampson, who had formerly been with the H.B.C. at Fort Rupert. Sampson and his Indian wife Lucy settled in the Fernwood district on the northeast shore of the island, near St. Mary Lake, while Booth took land on both sides of the tidal inlet that later became known as Booth Canal, south of Vesuvius.

Sampson was joined at Fernwood by Jonathan Begg and Edward

John Patton Booth. (COURTESY BC ARCHIVES)

Walker. In December Begg opened a general store, plant nursery and post office. Begg obtained the agency for fruit trees from established nurseries in California and Oregon. Advertising in the *New Westminster Times* in December 1859, Begg said he would be selling groceries, drygoods and hardware, but "positively no credit will be given." He added: "All goods will be sold for cash, at Victoria prices, cost of transportation added [but] all sorts of produce, such as shingles, deer, grouse, furs, etc., taken in exchange for goods."[6]

Begg's property became the hub of a settlement known as Beggsville, and his store was later renamed the Balmoral Store. In May 1861, it was raided by Haidas in 20 canoes, who took blankets, clothing and provisions. The Indians were caught soon after by the gunboat H.M.S. *Forward*. There was a move to have Sampson, with his knowledge of the Indians and their languages, named a special constable for the island, but Douglas took no action. The settlers began to arm themselves, taking guns into their fields and shooting back at night when shots were fired at their cabins. It was not until April of 1872 that Sampson was made a constable.

In 1860 a Victoria merchant, J.D. Cusheon, took over 1,000 acres of land surrounding the lake which bears his name. Cusheon brought over a gang of 16 men who spent four months clearing land, erecting a house and building a three-mile road to Ganges Harbour. In 1860, however, when Cusheon sought to obtain title to the land for $1.25 an acre, he was advised that he was entitled to pre-empt the maximum 200 acres but would have to pay five dollars an acre for any more land than that. Cusheon abandoned all the property and his ambitious plans, apparently in frustration over the colony's still-confused land policy.[7]

There was an election for the Legislative Assembly in 1860 and John Copland, the man who had precipitated the Salt Spring settlement, was nominated by ten islanders to represent the riding. Despite the support of De Cosmos in the *Colonist*, Copland lost to J.J. Southgate, a Victoria merchant. There were protests of irregularities in the Salt Spring voting registration and ballot-counting, but to no avail. An angry and disappointed Copland returned with his wife to Scotland, where they remained.

Because of the faulty registration, the only one of Copland's nominators able to cast a ballot was Edward Mallandaine, a member of the original band of 17 settlers. Mallandaine had pre-empted land on the eastern shore at Walker Hook, just south of Fernwood. He stayed there until April of 1863 when his house was vandalized by burglars. Mallandaine returned to Victoria, where he opened a school, set up in business as an architect, and published the first city directories, among other commercial activities.

In the spring of 1860, German-born Theodore Trage arrived on the island with a countryman, Harry Spikerman. Trage settled at Beaver Point, where he grew apples and strawberries and ran sheep. At first he took his produce to Cadboro Bay, and then switched to Sidney. Also that spring, the Salt Spring Island Agricultural Association was formed to help farmers market their output of butter, eggs, chicken, lamb and beef. Its creation was spearheaded by Jonathan Begg, John Booth and Tom Lineker.

The settlers were able to buy young fruit trees and ornamental shrubs from Begg's nursery, which carried a stock of apple, pear, plum, and cherry trees, as well as a variety of berries. Begg also offered to exchange groceries, clothing and hardware for fresh produce.

By May 8, 1861, there were 26 households in the area to the north of Ganges Harbour, known as the Central settlement, of which 17 belonged to Blacks. There were another 17 homes at Beggsville. After the unusually severe winter of 1861-62, a third of the settlers gave up. An estimated hundred head of cattle were lost because of the heavy snowfall and a lack of hay. Some farm animals also fell prey to wolves and cougars. (The wolves were eradicated by 1877, but cougars continued to plague the island for many years.) Freight service was irregular and provisions often ran short. Continuing Indian attacks and cattle rustling also discouraged the pioneers. Worst of all, for some of the lonely settlers, was the lack of mail service during the winter months.

Despite these setbacks, the development of the island continued. The first church service was held in 1861 by a Methodist preacher, Ebenezer Robson, brother of the pioneer newspaperman and future premier, John Robson. Ebenezer Robson came by canoe from Burrard Inlet, where he had settled after moving west from Ontario.

Boarding with John Booth, Reverend Robson made a point of visiting all the homes on the island.

Other itinerant ministers followed. In 1862 Salt Spring became part of the Anglican Diocese of Saanich under the Reverend R.W. Lowe, who made irregular visits. There was no church on the island until the building of St Paul's Catholic Church at Fulford Harbour in 1880.

The first school was established in 1861, in a log cabin near Ganges. The first teacher was John C. Jones. Four sons of a freed slave, Allen Jones, had graduated from Oberlin College in Ohio, and John had acquired a teacher's certificate. His brother Elias moved back to the U.S. from Salt Spring and William went to the Cariboo, where he practised as a dentist and invested in mining ventures. John Jones taught three days a week at the south end of the island, then walked to Beggsville to teach another three days.[8]

Jones served without pay for the first eight years, neglecting his own farm, but was given food and goods by the parents of his pupils. In 1864 the Ganges settlers petitioned Victoria to grant salaries to Jones and his assistant, Frederick Lester, but their appeal was ignored. Not until 1869, when a three-man school board made up of Booth, Thomas Griffiths and Abraham Copeland became the island's first elected political body, was Jones granted an annual salary of $500. Jones stayed until the mid-1870s when he returned to Oberlin, married and moved to his old home in North Carolina to teach for 25 years.

Among the Black pioneers of Salt Spring were Louis and Sylvia Stark. Sylvia Estes was born a slave in Missouri but the owner of her father and mother moved west and allowed the Estes to buy their freedom. Sylvia went with her family to California, where she met and married dairy farmer Louis Stark, the mixed-blood son of a woman slave and her white owner. In 1860 the couple and their four-year-old son Willis, along with Sylvia's parents, Howard and Hannah, moved north to Victoria, where a daughter, Emma, was born. Howard Estes bought a farm in Saanich; Louis Stark went to Salt Spring and built a cabin while Sylvia and the two children waited in Victoria to join him.

The Starks arrived at Vesuvius Bay on the schooner *Black*

Diamond in 1860 and pre-empted land to the north, near what is now Broadwell Mountain. A second son, John, was born soon after their arrival. A herd of 14 dairy cattle and chickens also came with them. At first, the two crates of eggs they produced each week paid for groceries. The chickens ran loose but Sylvia soon found their nesting places. Louis made most of their basic tools, including a plow fashioned from a v-shaped tree.[9]

When Reverend Robson visited the Starks about 18 months after their arrival he found that their dairy herd had doubled in number and they were growing wheat and vegetables. Sylvia "filled my sacks with good things," Robson wrote in his diary, "4 lbs fine fresh butter, 2 qt. bottles new milk. Mr. Stark gave me some of his large turnips."[10]

The Starks continued to prosper until a renewed wave of violence in the late 1860s caused them to move. In the spring of 1868 William Robinson, a Black pioneer who taught Sunday school in the Central settlement and worked on the Stark farm, was murdered. He was shot in the back while eating his supper in his small cabin on the Starks' property.

Another Black, Giles Curtis, replaced Robinson as a labourer for Stark and moved into the same cabin. Eight months later Curtis too was shot from behind and his throat cut with a knife. In July 1869, a Cowichan Indian was hanged at Chemainus for Curtis's murder on the dubious evidence of an Indian girl.

The Stark family was frightened and demoralized by the two killings. No other workers would come to the farm and Louis decided to move to a less isolated spot near Ganges, which they named Fruitvale. In 1873 Louis moved again, this time to the Cranberry district south of Nanaimo where he pre-empted 160 acres and proceeded to build up a farm. Sylvia joined him after two years, along with some of the children. Emma became a teacher in Cedar and John settled down to farm there after trying his hand at prospecting.

In 1896, when Louis was 85, he was found dead at the bottom of a cliff, apparently murdered. It was a tragic end for a man who had spent much of his life avoiding violence. The crime had nothing to do with race: the motive was greed for the coal deposits that were believed to lie under his land. Next to Stark's farm was the property of Ephraim Hodgson, a right-hand man of the mining tycoon, James Dunsmuir. "It was often Hodgson who was sent to deal with recalcitrant homesteaders whose land lay in Dunsmuir's way or whose pre-emption entitled them to a part of the coal Dunsmuir regarded as his sole preserve."[11]

Not long after Stark turned down an offer from Hodgson to buy his land and mineral rights, the old man's body was found—by Hodgson. The evidence presented to a coroner's inquest was contradictory and when the police took no action, John Stark hired a private detective to investigate the circumstances of his father's death. Six months after the body was discovered, Hodgson was arrested and charged with murder. There was little direct evidence implicating him, however, and he was released by Magistrate Mark Bate at a preliminary hearing. Hodgson later became a provincial policeman, and the murder of Louis Stark was never solved.

Sylvia (now known affectionately as "Aunt Silvey") returned to Salt Spring, where she lived to the age of 106, dying in 1944. Willis had stayed behind on Salt Spring to look after Fruitvale, and became a noted cougar hunter.

Although inter-racial marriages were common on Salt Spring—one Black family said all its boys married white girls, while the girls wed white boys—it is noteworthy that the Starks remained opposed to inter-racial marriages.

After the initial settlements were established at Central and Beggsville, newcomers started moving into the Fulford Valley-Burgoyne Bay area. In 1861 John Maxwell and his partner James Lunney sailed into Burgoyne Bay on their schooner and began farming with a hundred imported Texas longhorn cattle. Like so many others, the Irish-born Maxwell came to B.C. by way of the California gold rush and married an Indian woman. He planted an orchard and grain fields on his 1,000 acres. The first post office on Salt Spring was in the Maxwell home at Burgoyne Bay, and John's son Sam was the first postmaster.

Maxwell was continually plagued by Indian cattle rustlers who sold the meat in Nanaimo. In 1867 he and Michael Greavy of Mayne protested to Victoria about the lack of protection. They were supported by the *Colonist*, which said law on the Gulf Islands was a mockery. Farmers were at the mercy of marauders, both Indian and white, the newspaper said. They had paid for their land and deserved protection; otherwise they would be forced to take the law into their own hands. When the government failed to act, the stubborn Maxwell, Lunney and others in the valley did. An expert shot, Maxwell was opposed on principle to vigilante action, but decided there was no alternative if his ranch was to survive.

Later that year they set an ambush for the rustlers and fired on a number of Cowichans accompanied by a white man, none other than the infamous John McCawley. As they fled, the Indians apparently blamed McCawley for leading them into a trap. They slit his throat and threw the body into Sansum Narrows, an end in keeping with his double-dealing career. It was also the end of cattle rustling in the area, and Baynes Peak overlooking the valley was known forever after as Mount Maxwell.

Joseph Akerman had been a market gardener in England before coming to Victoria, where he established a vegetable plot on the site of the future Legislative Buildings. He moved to Salt Spring in 1861 and cleared a homestead beside Fulford Creek. Two years later

Martha Akerman. (COURTESY BC ARCHIVES)

he went to Victoria to meet the "bride ship" *Robert Lowe* from London and picked out Martha Clay to be his wife, the second white woman on Salt Spring. Martha proved a wise choice, a hard worker who bore seven children and lived to 99. On at least two occasions she was called on to scare off a cougar, once with piercing screams while waving a broom as the big cat stalked one of her children.

The Akermans developed a model farm, and Joe, a friendly, optimistic man, became a community leader. Succeeding generations of Akermans have continued to live in the valley, including Ted, who was born there in 1873. Ted Akerman was a road foreman and served as justice of the peace for 45 years. Joe and Martha also held the distinction of owning the first inn on the island, opening their home to paying guests and calling it "Traveller's Rest."[12]

Another early Burgoyne settler was Michael Gyves, an Irish Catholic who arrived in 1864 in Victoria, where he met his countryman, John Maxwell, who persuaded Gyves to settle near him in the Burgoyne Valley. Gyves pre-empted 200 acres on each side of Fulford Creek, and soon married the daughter of a Cowichan Indian chief. They had three children, two daughters and a son. Gyves supplemented his farm income by cutting and marketing cedar shakes.

Farmers attempting to grow crops in the valley had a hard time of it. "I cannot say much for the land," wrote surveyor Ashdown Green in 1874, "it being mostly gravel and salal." The ground was "very rocky and precipitous," Green added, "worthless except perhaps for sheep, but it would require so many acres to keep one sheep that it would not pay to buy it." The surveyor wrote scornfully of seeing "a specimen of a Salt Spring Island farmer" with a quarter-acre garden. Others were trying to cultivate "a few hollows between the rocks." Green found pockets of loam in the valley, but "on the mountain a goat would have hard work to get about." It hardly seemed the paradise that some were proclaiming, but Green did note the presence of big trees suitable for timber, and an abundance of deer.[13]

As the population of the valley grew, there was a need for a school. Distances to the other island settlements were too great for the children to walk. A Norwegian, John C. "Johnny" Sparrow, donated land for a building and 21 pupils were enrolled in the first schoolhouse in the valley. On March 16, 1878, the secretary of the Burgoyne Bay School Board, John Maxwell, sent a plaintive letter to the provincial superintendent of education, John Jessop:

> Mr. Jessop
> Sir the school children is all well of the whopping cough please send us up a teacher as soon as possible.
>   Yours truly
>   John Maxwell.

Other early settlers farther up the west side of the island were the Portuguese brothers Estalon and Manuel Bittancourt. They came to the Vesuvius district in the 1860s with the encouragement of their countryman, John Norton, who had also settled there. The Bittancourts were an industrious pair and soon prospered. For his family of two sons and six daughters, Estalon built a big house which much later became the Vesuvius Bay Lodge, destroyed by fire in 1975. A nephew, Reid Bittancourt, operated a store and feed business and became known as an expert builder who erected a number of homes on the island. Later he became a Customs agent at Ganges. (The name "Betancourt" also appears in island history; one branch of the large family chose to spell it that way.)

As one of four Catholic families on Salt Spring at the time, the Bittancourts were active in the building of St. Paul's Church at Fulford Harbour. The project was supervised by Father Peter Rondeault, who worked with the Cowichan Indians and was involved, with Father Gustav Donckele, in the Kuper Island Indian school. Lumber for the church was transported from Cowichan to the wharf at Burgoyne Bay by canoe and hauled along the valley road by Bill Whims on a stone-boat with a team of oxen. The church was consecrated on May 10, 1885, by Bishop John B. Brondel and is still standing.

In 1872 Abraham Copeland acquired land at Vesuvius Bay and agreed to build the first wharf on the west side of the island suitable for the handling of cargo and passengers. It was in fact a public wharf held in trust for the residents of the area.

Meanwhile, at the southeast end of the island, Beaver Point, two settlers put down roots that have lasted for many years. The first, in the summer of 1872, was Henry Ruckle. He pre-empted 27 acres after arriving from Ontario. Larger parcels of land were acquired in 1880 and 1881 and over the years the Ruckle farm expanded to 1,196 acres.

In 1877 Henry married Anna Christensen, a widow, and they raised two girls, and two boys who stayed on the farm—Alfred, Anna's son by her first marriage, and Daniel. Henry was active in the development of the district, becoming road foreman, school trustee and postmaster. Before a wharf was built at Beaver Point in 1895, building and food supplies for their property and produce from the mixed farm were carried to and from Sidney and New Westminster by whaleboat and rowboat.

Alfred married Martha Helen Margison in 1906. They had no children. Both were musical; Helen was a pianist and Alfred played violins he crafted from maple which he cut and cured. He was also active in the island's agricultural organizations. In 1943 Alfred sold his half-interest in the farm to the family, but stayed on there with his woodworking and violin-making.

In 1973 the family sold the property, which includes 4 1/2 miles of waterfront, to the provincial government as a park for the below-market price of $750,000. Two hundred acres were set aside as a farming reserve. The popular camping and picnic site is now known as Ruckle Park.

Samuel and Emily Beddis, with Emily's brother Raffles Augustus Robert Purdy, arrived in Victoria in 1884 with their five children from the U.S., having left England 12 years before. Beddis bought a sloop, loaded his family and household goods aboard, and set off looking for a place to homestead. A storm drove them onto one of the San Juan Islands, where they were chased off by a U.S. Revenue agent. Returning to the Saanich Peninsula, they met Henry Ruckle, who persuaded the family to try the Beaver Point area. At that time there were only 12 white families on the island.

The Beddis family lived in a big tent warmed by a log fire in front of the open flaps while they built a log and timber house with Ruckle's assistance. A trail was cut through the woods to Ganges Harbour, but it was decided that a school was needed at Beaver

Students and teacher at the Beaver Point schoolhouse, ca *1887.*
(COURTESY BC ARCHIVES)

Point; Samuel, with his sons Charles and Henry, built a one-room
school in the spring of 1885 with lumber from Port Moody and
Cowichan. Henry and Charles were among the first 17 pupils. The
schoolhouse, still standing today, also served for a time as a community hall, for church services and meetings.

Hawaiian children from Russell and Portland islands, including
some members of the Naukana family, attended the school by boat.
Margaret Jackson was the first teacher. Subsequent teachers included George Kirkendale, who became Victoria Harbour Master,
and K.C. Symons, later principal of St. Michael's School in Victoria.

Beddis set to work planting an apple orchard with 40 varieties
mailed from Ireland as slender grafts embedded in potatoes. The
winter of 1893 was another severe one, with six feet of snow on the
ground, and Samuel was stricken by pneumonia. When it became
apparent that he needed hospital care, his wife, his two eldest sons
and an uncle wrapped him in blankets and a tarpaulin, placed him in
an open boat and rowed to Victoria. The trip took from mid-
afternoon to seven A.M. the next morning. Samuel was taken to hos-

pital in Victoria but died there, at the age of 43. The sons now took over the running of the property. Their mother returned to the farm to give birth to the last child, Geoffrey, a month later. Emily went on to help other families in isolated homesteads with her nursing skills, reaching them by hiking or rowboat.[14]

The only resident doctor in the early days was John Hogg, a retired M.D. from England who was compelled into practice by the lack of medical care on the island. Handicapped by the loss of an arm, Hogg lived alone in a small house overlooking the Harbour House site at the head of Ganges Harbour. He was later killed by an Indian he had caught stealing his turnips.

After the Beddis family's arrival on Salt Spring, Raffles Purdy had gone to Central to teach, staying from 1885 to 1897 when he started a farm and apple orchard off Beddis Road near the sea, with the help of Japanese workers. In 1911, at the age of 50, he was married to a woman he had met during a trip home to England, and had three daughters. They lived in a waterfront home with an orchard on Ganges Harbour. When no clergyman was on hand for Sunday service, Purdy served as a lay reader.[15]

In 1868 Salt Spring and the other southern Gulf Islands became part of the Electoral District of Cowichan. The island's first representative in the Legislative Assembly at Victoria was John Booth, who later became Speaker of the House. After his election in 1871 Booth asked the province for $1,000 for roads and $1,000 for schools on the island. That simple request turned out to be the first shot in a battle that would divide the islanders into bitter factions for the next ten years and beyond. "At the best of times there seems to have been a certain amount of mutual distrust between the different communities of settlers on the island, and the question of roads always brought to light diverse opinions, which increased the distrust and at times created an atmosphere of open hostility."[16]

Two years later Letters Patent were issued for the incorporation of the Township of Salt Spring Island. Seven men were elected to the first council, including the teacher, John Jones, and Henry W. Robinson, who became clerk. Booth later became reeve. The first meeting, on January 30, 1873, passed a number of municipal by-laws, and the troubles began.

The bylaws established a road committee, with payments of $2.75 a day to foremen and inspectors; tradesmen were required to obtain a licence to operate their business, with fines up to $25 for non-compliance; and "for the improvement of cattle it shall not be lawful for any bull to run at large during the months of April, May and June." A five-dollar fine would be levied for each offence.

When it became known that the council had incurred an immediate debt of $300 for miscellaneous expenditures, a number of farmers were outraged. Branding the councillors "tyrants," they signed documents and petitions declaring they had not understood the ramifications of incorporation. The dissidents declared that 30 landholders would have to bear the burden of taxation. Ninety percent of the islanders were claimed to be opposed to incorporation because it would result in the imposition of taxes.

Apart from the direct issue of taxation, the dispute boiled down to different visions of Salt Spring's future—boosters of spending for growth and development projects opposed by defenders of the status quo. That kind of conflict is still rampant today, on Salt Spring and the other Gulf Islands, as well as in communities all over the province. It is particularly vociferous on the islands because of the individualistic nature of many settlers, which brought them there in the first place.

The incorporation dispute simmered through the 1870s, then heated up in the early 1880s. At the centre were four Pimbury brothers, Edwin, John, Philip and Augustus, English-born sheepranchers who moved from Cobble Hill to become the first settlers in the Musgrave district on the southwest section of the island. Edwin, who served two terms in the Legislative Assembly for Cowichan riding between 1875 and 1882, later went to Nanaimo, where he became a druggist. There were two other brothers in England. Of the four in B.C., all remained bachelors except Augustus, who married late. John died on Salt Spring, while Augustus and Phillip returned to the Cowichan district.

The Pimbury property was a large, remote holding on the slopes of Mount Tuam, on which they had not expected to pay taxes since it was a long way from any services. A year after the bylaws were passed, the Pimburys complained to Lieutenant-Governor Joseph

Trutch that the councillors were receiving public money illegally. (Clerk Robinson was paid $2.75 per diem and others got small amounts for road inspections. Reeve Booth was also alleged to have taken $20 for his own use.)

Fred Foord, who had settled on Salt Spring in 1864, became the island's first justice of the peace and later treasurer of the council. He told the provincial cabinet in 1881 that the Pimburys had been leading a crusade against municipal governments because they wanted to avoid paying any taxes. The Pimburys, supported by 19 other settlers, including John Maxwell and Michael Gyves, succeeded in overturning a civic election in 1881 by launching a suit against Henry Robinson in his role as returning officer. Reeve Booth and the other councillors saw the battle was lost, and in May of 1883 offered no resistance when the legislature annulled the letters patent and the municipality was dissolved.

Not all the violence on Salt Spring in the last century was instigated by Indians. A brutal murder involving a love triangle shocked the settlers a week before Christmas in 1891.

John K. Brown had lived on the island for 15 years, but spent frequent periods of from four to 12 months in England, where he owned considerable property. At home on the island, he lived with his second wife, Jane Melinda. During her husband's absences, the neighbours noted that their handyman, Jim Darrington, spent more than his usual amount of time at the three-room house, often staying overnight. Both Mrs. Brown and Darrington, a strong, muscular man, were known to be heavy drinkers.

On December 17 Jane told her neighbour, Fred Foord, that Brown was planning to sell the Salt Spring property and leave her on her own. Foord testified later that Brown had told him previously that he did plan to sell out and move back to England without his wife, but would pay her monthly support.

Another neighbour, Arthur Cartwright, said he went to the house on the morning of the 18th and was told by Mrs. Brown that her husband was dead. She said he had apparently suffered a stroke or heart attack and had fallen and hit his head on the bricks of the hearth. Cartwright said she seemed unconcerned, and that Darrington was sleeping at the time on a bunk in the kitchen. Both had been drinking.

A trail of blood was found between Brown's body and the bedroom. It was apparent that the body had been dragged on a bloodstained piece of carpet into the living-room. Dr. Wymond W. Walkem found finger marks on Brown's throat, indicating he had been strangled. Darrington and Jane Brown were charged with murder and jailed in Nanaimo to await trial. The Assizes were set for June, but in April Darrington obtained a knife and killed himself by slitting his throat.

A jury convicted Mrs. Brown on a reduced charge of manslaughter after the prosecution said "mercy" should be shown, and she should be given the benefit of the doubt whether or not Darrington had committed the actual killing. (A Constable Maxwell had testified, however, that on the Sunday after the murder he heard Darrington say to Jane: "You killed Brown," and that she had made no reply.) Before being sentenced to five years, Jane Brown told Judge Henry Crease: "I am not guilty, my Lord."[17]

It would be some years before Salt Spring had a full-fledged hotel, but around the turn of the century the place for itinerant preachers, teachers and bachelors to stay was the Stevens Boarding House. Built about 1887 in the Central settlement by Henry Stevens and his wife Anne, the boxy, two-storey house stood for more than a century. Their nephew Walter Stevens later took over the boarding-house and adjacent farm.

Raffles Purdy stayed there when he went to Central to teach, paying the usual one dollar a day for bed and board. Another notable boarder was Reverend Edward Francis Wilson. He stayed there in 1894 while waiting for a house to be built for his wife Fanny and their ten children in Victoria, as well as two young Indian girls they cared for.

Wilson had left England in 1868 to enter missionary service in central Canada. He founded a number of schools for Indian youths in communities stretching from Sarnia to Medicine Hat. Wilson became an authority on Indian culture and language, writing two books on the subject, and ministered to the Metis imprisoned after the Riel Rebellion. He came to the coast in 1893 and served briefly with the Anglican Church in Victoria before moving to Salt Spring.

Wilson first arrived at Vesuvius on Sunday morning, February 4, 1894, from Victoria, after staying overnight on Kuper Island. He hiked across to Central and held a service at three P.M. for 22 people in St. Mark's Anglican Church, which is still standing. The church was built on an acre of land donated by the Stevens in 1889 at the top of the hill above the boarding-house. It was constructed with voluntary labour and donated materials, supervised by Samuel Beddis and his son Charles, who stayed at the boarding-house during construction. The first Anglican church on the island, it was consecrated in 1892. The boarding-house was used for parish meetings.

After staying overnight with the Stevens, Reverend Wilson returned to Victoria and was offered the Salt Spring parish by Bishop William W. Perrin. He was back on the island within a week. "I very soon made up my mind that Salt Spring was to be our home," he wrote in his diary. For his homesite Wilson chose the old 100-acre Armstead Buckner farm at Central. He bought it from Victoria financier and land speculator Joe Boscowitz, who was asking $1,200 but accepted less for cash.[18]

In his diary Wilson described the farm as mostly bush and swamp and a "rickety old log house with a mud chimney." The doors had been left open "and cattle and sheep had evidently been in and out at will." The house was too small for his large brood, so Wilson took apart an addition which had been put on his house in Victoria and shipped it to Salt Spring to enlarge the old Buckner house. It was carried by tug and barge to Vesuvius and carted 2 1/2 miles to the property by wagon. Wilson also brought over some fruit trees from his Victoria place before selling it. The family was ensconced in their new home by Christmas. It was called "Barnsbury," after Wilson's ancestral home, Barnsbury Park, in Islington, England.

In addition to working on the house, Wilson had a busy year in 1894. On May 24 he took part in May Day celebrations at Cusheon Lake with 200 island residents, but found them too "frivolous" for his austere taste. On June 30 a second Anglican church, St. Mary's at Fulford, was consecrated by Bishop Perrin on land donated by Johnny Sparrow. On September 13 a concert was held in the old

Central schoolhouse to raise funds for St. Mark's, and a total of $55 was donated by 120 concert-goers.

A big man, black-bearded and often bad-tempered, Wilson was an accomplished surveyor, artist and writer. He provided medical care to the Indians and others before a resident physician, Dr. Gerald Baker, arrived in 1898; Wilson solicited funds from the islanders to buy medical supplies. Travelling around the island by horse and buggy, he always carried a rug because on some nights after service, he curled up to sleep on a pew. He kept a log of his trips around the island, which usually totalled about 2,000 miles annually.

On March 1, 1902, Wilson conducted the funeral service for John Booth, one of the island's most respected men, despite the incorporation furore. After serving for four years in the first legislature after B.C. joined Confederation, Booth confined himself to island affairs for 15 years until he was elected again in 1890 as the first member from the new riding of "The Islands." He was re-elected in '94, '98 and 1900. After marrying the widow of Thomas Griffiths, Booth moved from Booth Bay to her ranch at Fernwood overlooking Trincomali Channel. He was 64 when he died of Bright's disease. The funeral was the most impressive ever held on Salt Spring. Premier James Dunsmuir and 30 M.L.A.s attended the service, and the mourners included future premiers Richard McBride and John Oliver.

Wilson kept a meticulous record of Salt Spring affairs during most of his term as rector of the church. He began publishing the monthly newsletter *Parish and Home* in 1895, changed its name to *Church Monthly* in 1901 and continued until 1905. Wilson was both acerbic and humorous in his little news items. Noting that it was planned to put a small garden between the road and the entrance to St Mark's Church, he observed that "the congregation will have to make a slight detour over the rocks in order to get to the church door. Perhaps some will regard this as a good excuse for continuing their irregular attendance at the services."[19]

When an earthquake shook the island on January 3, 1896, "a gentleman in the agonies of toothache reprimanded his patient wife for attending to the earthquake instead of his face. The father of a family, thinking his house was going to collapse, ran out of doors and called to his wife to look after the children." When Klondike fever hit the island in 1898 Wilson advised the men to "stick to your farms... there is no fear of freezing to death here." Soon after that he noted without comment that his son Llewelyn had joined the exodus to the north.

Wilson took an informal census in 1895 with a racial and social breakdown of the island's population of under 450: There were 160 English or Canadians, 90 mixed-blood Indians, 50 Scots, 34 white Americans, 40 Blacks, 22 Portuguese, 20 Irish, ten Japanese and six Hawaiians. There were 62 married couples, 35 single men or widowers; 50 young men and 20 young women, and 180 children. By far the largest number of men, 105, were farmers. Ten fur-seal hunters who shipped out on schooners for the North Pacific each year made their homes on Salt Spring.

The largest landholder at that time was a Captain Trench, a non-resident, who had 4,000 acres suitable only for sheep on the old Musgrave estate. Edward Musgrave, the youngest son of an Irish baronet, had tried raising sheep in Argentina before acquiring 7,000 acres on the island. The family then moved across to the Cowichan

Front, l. to r. Arthur, Mrs. Wilson, Kathleen, Llewelyn, Nora, Reverend Wilson, Flossie, Winnie, Keith. Standing, l. to r. Evelyn, Bertie, Norman. (COURTESY BC ARCHIVES)

Valley in the 1890s, selling some of the land to Trench. The famed yachting couple, Miles and Beryl Smeeton, later lived on a portion of the original property. Other large properties included 2,500 acres of mountainous sheep-grazing land owned by W. Robertson, and the 1,260-acre Broadwell ranch. The Broadwells, Joel and Amanda, had come from Nanaimo to the Central settlement in 1882. Broadwell served as postmaster from 1885 to 1900 and was also justice of the peace. He grew black currants on his farm and in 1897 shipped more than a ton. Broadwell also dabbled in real estate, buying and selling old farms which he had spruced up, including the Fruitvale farm of Willis Stark. In 1902 he sold his own home to Ernest Crofton, who had married Henry Bullock's sister Mary.

As farming expanded on the mainland, with easier access to the new markets there, declining prices made most agriculture unprofitable on Salt Spring. The men turned to other pursuits, chiefly logging, which became the largest industry on the island by 1920. At one time there were 15 sawmills operating on Salt Spring, many cutting railway ties. That business slacked off too as timber supplies diminished.

Prospectors roamed the island's hills and creek beds hunting mineral deposits, but nothing of consequence came from their efforts. A few experimental salt borings were made near the springs at the north end which gave the island its name, a small amount of gold was extracted in the Beaver Point area around the turn of the century, and copper was found on Mount Maxwell. There was a small quartz mine briefly on Mount Bruce above the Musgrave wharf, and Estalon Bittancourt found some coal on his property which he sold for 25¢ a sack to islanders. About two tons were dug in 1896.

The first short telephone line was put up in 1897 and two years later there was a line running 13 miles from Vesuvius to Fulford, with 20 miles in total on the island. A cable from Vesuvius to Vancouver Island was laid in 1901 and the Ganges-Victoria connection was made in 1904.

Wilson served as rector of St. Mark's for 15 years until his retirement in 1911. He gave each of his five boys ten-acre parcels of land for homes. In the 1920s Norman Wilson started the golf club.

W.A. "Theo" Burkitt bought 40 acres of land on St. Mary Lake in 1920 from the Mouat family where he raised pigs, cows and horses, and had a few fruit trees. In the 1930s Burkitt developed a resort and fishing camp on the lake which he later sold. A founding member of the golf club, he vowed in 1939 not to play another round until the Germans had been beaten, which turned out to be a long layoff.

All five Wilson daughters were married to Salt Spring men: Evelyn to Charles Tolson, Florence to George Borradaile, Kathleen to Frank Scott, Evelyn to F.H. Walter, and Nora to Fred Crofton. Recapping the events of the previous years in 1905, Wilson noted that "of weddings there have been few, my own family furnishing the majority."

When Fred Crofton arrived on the island from Ireland in 1898, the vicarage was the social centre of the Central settlement, especially for young bachelors enamoured of the Wilson daughters. After marrying Nora, Crofton farmed for a time at the head of Ganges Harbour and was joined by his brothers Ernest and Frank. In 1902 Fred became proprietor of the Harbour House Hotel, and when he joined up in 1916 Nora took over the hotel, helped by her brother Norman. They got a licence to serve beer the following year. There were 11 rooms in the hotel and tents on the grounds in the summer. Harbour House was owned by the Crofton family until 1964.[20]

Frank Scott was one of four brothers from England who came to Salt Spring in the 1880s and '90s. The others were Harold, William and Geoffrey. Six other brothers remained in England. The Scotts were ardent supporters of Reverend Wilson and the church. In 1899 Wilson acknowledged a donation to himself by William in hay and wheat worth $25, and Geoffrey gave ten dollars in cash.

Frank developed an apple orchard near Ganges. William bought 700 acres at Fruitvale in 1891, near the present Scott Point named after him, where he planted 1,200 fruit trees and raised dairy cattle. A justice of the peace, he was later appointed to the provincial Board of Horticulture. Geoffrey served as chairman of the board of the Salt Spring Island Creamery for 43 years. Harold drowned in a boating mishap in Ganges Harbour with his friend Fred Smedley in February of 1898, just a week after playing the Wedding March for his brother Frank and Kathleen Wilson. "Some of the white roses that had been used at the wedding were used again at the funeral," Reverend Wilson noted sadly.[21]

After his retirement, Reverend Wilson lived briefly in California before returning to Victoria, where he died in 1915, aged 71.

There could have been no more unlikely guest at the Stevens Boarding House over the years than Henry Wright ("Harry" to the unintimidated) Bullock, the subject of endless gossip, who became known as the "Squire of Salt Spring." The 12-room mansion Bullock built was the social focus of the island during his 54 years' residence, despite (or because of) his bachelorhood. Many did not quite know what to make of him at the time, but he has passed into Salt Spring legend as a beloved eccentric. Today's historians might cast a more questioning gaze on his peccadillos.

The son of a clergyman in Buckinghamshire, England, Bullock arrived on Salt Spring in 1892 at the age of 24 with an apparently bottomless wallet. After buying a 220-acre property from Eric and Nels Nelson on what became known as Bullock's Lake, a mile from Ganges, Bullock settled into the boarding-house for five years while Reid Bittancourt supervised the building of his house. Japanese labourers were paid 50¢ a day to erect fences, and plant fruit, nut and ornamental trees along his curving driveway, and lawns sloping toward the lake. His goal was to create a gracious English estate on Salt Spring's rocky hills. It seemed a long way from the time just a few decades before when Indians battled on the beach not far away.

Before settling into his role of social lion, Bullock set to work establishing a model farm. Dairy cattle, chickens, corn and asparagus flourished on the property. The latest mechanical devices were installed: a steam engine was employed to thresh grain; a gasoline engine generated electricity for power and lighting, the first on the island; and the mansion's indoor plumbing was also a first.

But it was his sumptuous parties, balls, dinners and luncheons that made Bullock the talk of the island. The squire took it upon himself to instruct the rustic Salt Spring folk on the niceties of dress and deportment. A portly, bearded figure who favoured a long black frock coat, silk top hat, bow tie and gloves, Bullock expected his male guests to conform to a similar standard.

It was the ladies, however, who received his most doting attention, especially the socially aspiring younger belles. He encouraged them all to wear earrings and gave pairs to those daring enough to submit to having their ears pierced with darning needles. The young women were persuaded to cinch up their corsets to the 18-inch waists that accentuated the fashionable hour-glass figure. Five-inch spiked heels were also encouraged, which proved a challenge to the farm girls. Bullock's favourites were presented with gifts of fans, white gloves and veils to add to their allure. When Bullock died and his safe was opened, inside with a large sum of money were drawers of white gloves, veils and pearl earrings.

Bullock made sure that everyone had enough to drink at his parties to make them pleasantly tipsy. The rule of the house was sherry with everything. His seven-course dinners included a spoonful in most of the dishes, with a bit extra for the oxtail soup. After the ball was over, Bullock insisted his guests take a "stirrup cup" of spirits for the ride home.

A man of Falstaffian appetites in his younger days, Bullock would invite 25 guests for dinner at two sittings and would eat at both. The main courses were formidable—14-pound roasts cut into three or four thick servings and huge platters of halibut. Despite his elegant manners, Bullock was seen on occasion to use his fork as a comb to remove food from his bushy beard.

Bullock also brought a number of London slum youths out from Dr. Thomas Barnardo's homes. They were given lessons in both farming and deportment. For service in the house, including waiting on table, they were supplied with button-decorated Eton suits.

One such recipient of Bullock's beneficence was Jesse Bond, who came from the Protestant Orphanage in Victoria in 1906 at the age of 12. Jesse served as houseboy at first, and then was taught to cook. Bullock didn't believe boys "of his class" needed further schooling, but during his nine years with Bullock, young Bond learned about farming and when he showed an interest in photography, he was given a camera. After going off to the First World War, Bond returned to Salt Spring and tried mixed farming and logging before settling into a 300-acre property on which he developed a market garden. A number of boys who stayed on the island after service

Henry Bullock. (COURTESY BC ARCHIVES)

with Bullock were given plots of land to start farming.

Bullock was not always a benevolent master, however. He frequently took a cane or switch to boys he considered guilty of misbehaviour, and his method of teaching them to swim was primitive: he sat in his boat holding a long pole to which the boys were attached by belts.

Besides his "poor" boys, Bullock ran a boarding-school for the sons of gentlemen who could afford to pay $250 a year. These boys, aged nine to 14, lived in a dormitory behind the house and were also taught farming and deportment. Part of their ritual was an early-morning parade before breakfast on the mansion's 60-foot verandah.

In the early days Bullock travelled around the island's 48 miles of roadways in a horse-drawn buggy with one of the boys holding the reins. Then he acquired a 1912 Model-T Ford, the second on the island. Jesse Bond and other boys spent many hours cleaning and polishing the vehicle for Sunday's ceremonial trips to St. Mark's Church, to which Bullock had donated land for a vicarage. After the car collided with an ox-cart, some residents complained that it was scaring their horses. They asked Bullock to keep it off the road on boat-days, and days when the farmers made deliveries to the creamery. If he must use the car, they said, would he please have a man walking in front with a red flag warning of its coming. When he went into the village on "clear" days, Bullock sent a boy ahead to warn horse owners of his noisy arrival.

It was during a frustrating day in Ganges that Bullock decided to go into the merchandise business. After following his usual custom of sending one of his boys into Mouat's general store for supplies, Bullock sat fuming while the boy was delayed. It is said that Bullock became so enraged that he decided to start a rival store, The Gulf Island Trading Company, in partnership with T.F. Speed and the Scott brothers. Bullock already had one foot in business with his importing firm, the India Tea Company, based in Vancouver, which was a most profitable enterprise. After Bullock died in 1946 at the age of 79, the new store carried on until 1969, when it was bought out by the Mouats, Salt Spring's most enterprising family dynasty.

There were seven Mouat brothers born on the main island of the Shetlands. The first to arrive on Vancouver Island was Thomas, who in 1894 with his wife Jane went to Nanaimo where they had relatives and friends. (Captain William A. Mouat, who arrived on the coast in 1845 and was the skipper of a number of H.B.C. steamers, was no relation.) In Nanaimo the brothers met Joel Broadwell, who told them about a property for sale on Salt Spring.

The following year they bought the farm of Abraham Copeland near St. Mary Lake. Tom was only 45 when he died in 1898, leaving his widow with 11 children to care for. One of the boys, Gilbert, who a few years later was to be stricken with polio, worked for the Malcolm & Purvis Store at Ganges. Joseph Malcolm and Percy Purvis were two Americans who had built up a thriving business, mostly the result of Purvis's energy and skills. Purvis had a ranch a mile and a half from the village and developed an export business in conjunction with the store. They bought produce from island farmers to sell in Ladysmith, shipped on their powerboat the *Nomad* and later the *Ganges*. They hoped to get better prices for meat and fresh fruit and vegetables there than in Victoria.[22]

In 1907 Gilbert Mouat, "a born salesman," learned that the store was up for sale, following Malcolm's death. Mouat's mother raised the money, and the trading firm of G.J. Mouat & Co. came into being. At that time Jane Mouat moved from St. Mary Lake to Ganges to take charge of the store. Another son, William, joined the firm and the name was changed to Mouat Brothers Company. A new store, built in 1912, is still standing by the harbour. Jane, later known as "Granny Mouat," ran the Ganges Inn in the old store beside the new building.

In 1903 the Mouats, Scotts and Henry Bullock put up money to build the island's first creamery. The distinctive stone building was located at Ganges and now houses a bakery. Farmers on all the Gulf Islands shipped their dairy products to the creamery, which became a substantial Salt Spring business.

Some 200,000 quarts of pasteurized milk were delivered annually to Victoria from the creamery. The peak year was 1928 when 140,000 pounds of butter were shipped, with cream coming from 136 farms. A.W. Drake was the chief butter-maker for 37 years, from 1912 to 1949. Geoffrey Scott was chairman from the opening in 1904 until his retirement in 1947. The creamery stayed in business until 1957 when costly new government regulations were introduced and many of the islands' pioneer dairy farmers had retired or died. Butter production had dropped to 30,000 pounds.

Gavin Colvin Mouat was born to Thomas and Jane in Nanaimo in 1893 and became the family's most successful businessman. He was involved in real estate, timber and the Gulf Islands Ferry Company, of which he was president.

During and after the war Gavin Mouat was at the centre of controversy over the removal of Japanese-Canadians from the Gulf Islands, and the subsequent seizure and sale of their property. He was appointed by the federal government as custodian of "alien property" on the islands and supervised their sale. Although not as numerous as on Mayne, Japanese-Canadians had settled on Salt Spring. Kumanosuko Okano and his wife Riyo moved to the island in 1920 after fishing out of Crofton. They developed an extensive market garden in the Booth Canal valley and built the first large greenhouse on the island. Katsuyeri and Kimiko Murakami were another of the 12 Japanese-Canadian families on the island on December 7, 1941, when the Pacific war started. They lost all their personal possessions during internment, and the sale of their land and buildings after the war realized less than $500, about one-tenth of their value. The family returned to the island, however.

But the most troublesome case was that of the Torazo Iwasaki family. A naturalized citizen, Iwasaki in the 1920s had bought 640 acres of waterfront property near Vesuvius with a valuable stand of timber. By 1940 he and his wife Fuku had paid off the $4,000 purchase price. Two years later they were shipped off to an internment camp at Greenwood in the B.C. interior after being given two hours to pack their belongings.

In 1945 Iwasaki was advised by Ottawa that his property had been sold to Gavin Mouat for $5,250. Like a number of other Japanese-Canadian victims, Iwasaki refused to recognize the sale and submitted a claim for $66,000 to a federal commission set up under Justice Henry I. Bird to hear their cases. Bird fixed a value of $12,000 on the Iwasaki property and awarded them an additional $8,000. Iwasaki reluctantly signed an official release. He made a number of protests to Ottawa during the next few years, but to no avail.[23]

As the fastest growing and most populous—by far—of the Gulf Islands, Salt Spring has always been viewed with a mix of envy and scorn by its poorer neighbours. With a resident population today of more than 7,000, the process of urbanization has grown swiftly in recent decades. This change was accelerated after the end of the Second World War, when the population jumped by one-third within a few years to 2,500. From the start of settlement in 1859 up to the First World War, farming and logging had been the mainstays of Salt Spring's economy. Logging has continued in a small way, but the trend has been steadily toward service industries catering to retirees, artists and craftspeople.

Lavender, Missions
and Brown Swiss Cattle

Lying just north of Salt Spring, across Houstoun Pass, are the twin islands of Kuper and Thetis, each about ten square miles in size. Like the two Pender islands, they were originally joined by a shallow strip of land. In 1905, about the same time as on Pender, a canal was dug to allow small boats to pass through.

The waterway had a depth of only six feet at low tide, and even less at the rocky western entrance in Telegraph Harbour. This obstruction caused the canal to silt up over time. A bridge linked the two islands for some years but was knocked down in 1946. Neither island was satisfied with the new partial separation. The Indians of Kuper were angered when their horses, cows and sheep crossed over at low tide to Thetis and were occasionally shot by residents frustrated over the destruction of their crops.

The first Thetis landholder was Robert Foster, who took up 160-acre Lot 1 on April 3, 1873. He spent little time on the island and his land reverted to the Crown. Next came William Henry Curran, an Irishman who had arrived at Esquimalt in 1861 and settled in the Chemainus area. He became interested in the timber on Thetis and began pre-empting quarter-section lots in 1874. Curran logged with oxen for a number of years, towing the logs three miles across Stuart Channel to the Chemainus sawmill. After Curran was married to an Indian woman he had a large family, and over the years built three log houses in different parts of the island.[1]

Few settlers arrived during the 1880s other than Harvey Sitwell and H.E. Donald, two bachelors who cleared land at Telegraph Harbour to begin a farm, and Henry Severne, who bought at Preedy Harbour in 1884. The newcomers rowed across to Chemainus for groceries and mail. It was on one of these junkets in January 1891, that Henry Severne was drowned with a Chemainus hotelman, Sam Gray, when their boat overturned on the way back to Thetis. Severne's body was found on the beach, guarded by his collie, which had been in the boat and apparently dragged him ashore.

One of the numerous Shetland Island families which settled in the Gulf Islands, the Hunters, started on Thetis in 1891. Peter and his brother Joseph bought land first at North Cove, and later Peter moved to the west side where he built a new home in 1895. He built the 26-foot open sailing skiff *Sea Saucer* in 1893 and sailed and rowed over to the Fraser River with Joseph to fish each summer. On the island he used a team of oxen raised on his farm for plowing and other heavy work.

In 1897 Joseph was joined at North Cove by their 70-year-old mother, three brothers and a sister. They also used oxen for plowing, and specialized at first in growing tomatoes, as well as keeping the usual complement of farm animals. In 1896 Joseph and his brother got a $150 contract from the government to build a road from North Cove to Preedy Harbour. In later years the Hunter family expanded their sheep flock and also went into logging, fishing and whaling. In 1910 they built a 30-foot gasboat, the *Thetis*, to take farm produce to market on Vancouver Island and bring back supplies.

In 1892 Mr. and Mrs. Henry Burchell arrived on the island. They had come from England to Victoria two years earlier and lost most of their savings in a business venture. They had planned to make a new start on the Skeena River, but moved instead to Thetis, and scraped together enough money to buy the Preedy Harbour property from the Henry Severne estate. The Burchells gradually acquired a total of 1,300 acres, almost half the island. The other half belonged to the Hunters.

Settling at Preedy Harbour, the Burchells opened the first store on Thetis. Most of their customers were Indians, with whom Mrs. Burchell dealt by learning to speak Chinook. They usually bought one article at a time, for which they paid, took their change and began all over again. The Burchell store was one of the last to accept the traditional H.B.C. blanket as money. Burchell did other trade with the Indians, including the purchase of dogfish oil which he sold to the Nanaimo coal mines as a lubricant and lamp fuel. Many items were sold to the Indians for potlatches.

As well as managing their farm and orchard, this energetic couple also operated a sawmill, which cut most of the lumber used on the island. Some of it went into building the Burchells' spacious home, Preedy Hall. They joined the original log house with an adjacent unfinished frame house and put on numerous additions. Acetylene gas lamps were installed for lighting. There were seven bedrooms, a large music room for entertaining, and a private chapel, with stained-glass windows and some carved figures from Oberammergau, adjoining the house, and a tennis court on the grounds.[2]

Henry Burchell was a man of many talents, including architecture and carpentry, and he designed and carried out much of the work himself. He was also an accomplished linguist and ardent seaman, preferring his naphtha-powered launch *Sunbeam* to sailing craft.

Another endeavour of the Burchells was bringing out Englishmen, mostly young bachelors, to their property to learn the rudiments of farming, much like Henry Bullock on Salt Spring. The men lived in a dormitory building behind the house. Some of the pupils later settled around the Burchell property, while others went to work as farmhands on Vancouver Island or the other Gulf Islands, earning an average of $20 a month and board. Burchell and others went into the poultry business on a large scale for a time, but the difficulties in reaching markets and the outbreak of the First World War put an end to that enterprise. Out of a total island population of 70 people, 32 men enlisted in 1914. Seven were killed in action.

The Burchells nevertheless continued after the war to entertain in the grand manner. At Christmas Henry Burchell put on a Santa Claus suit and gave out presents to all the island children at a party in the big house. A special dance was held in the music room on the night of the first full moon after haying had been completed. Guests came from all over for the annual event, including the Paynes, who sailed and rowed from Saturna. They were fed oysters, chicken, salmon, cider and sparkling white wine. The last one was held in 1923, a year before Burchell died. In 1926 Mrs. Burchell sold the property to Hans Hunter, a mining engineer from Japan who was not related to the pioneer Hunter family on the island. Hunter's manager, a Mr. Gaitskell, was looking after the house when it burned down. A new Preedy Hall, still standing, was built around 1930.

As a result of the settlement of the Burchells' young farming stu-

Mr. and Mrs. Henry Burchell. (COURTESY BC ARCHIVES)

dents, who later sent for their relatives, Thetis became known as an English colony. Few of these, however, were more English in dress and style than Major Alfred Heneage and his sister Eveline Mary, who lived in a big house that eventually became the headquarters of Camp Columbia, an Anglican retreat for 40 years.

The major had been a career cavalry officer with the British army, trained at Sandhurst Military College, who had seen service in India and the Boer War. A member of an aristocratic Lincolnshire family, he had decided at 46 to retire to the B.C. coast. Arriving in Victoria in 1904, Heneage took the train to Courtenay, stopping along the way to ask questions about desirable places to settle. He heard about Thetis, where he bought 73 acres of waterfront on the west side facing Chemainus before returning to England to persuade Eveline to come out and keep house for him. They had been orphaned in childhood, along with two other brothers, and all were brought up separately. None ever married. Eveline was artistic and had gone to art college in England. She was withdrawn from the school, however, when her two spinster guardian aunts discovered she had been drawing nudes.

Alfred and Eveline lived in separate little primitive cottages on the beach while "Heneage House" was being built. The major hired Chinese labourers in Chemainus to clear land and work on the house. They came and went by boat each day. After the house was built, the Heneages always dressed for dinner, one at each end of their large dining-room table. The mail came from Chemainus only once a week by power launch, so the major decided in 1905 to buy his own powerboat. He knew nothing about engines and it broke down frequently. On such occasions he simply drifted and waited for rescuers to recognize his plight.

To occupy her time Eveline grew lavender which she distilled into lavender water in a small business enterprise. Patterned glass phials were imported from Italy as containers. Eveline showed her artistic skills in other unorthodox ways. On one visit to a garden party at Government House in Victoria, she wore a hat decorated with chicken feathers she had gathered in their henhouse run.

Both devout Anglicans, the Heneages had a minister travel from Chemainus once a month for services which were held in an upstairs bedroom or downstairs storeroom. Major Heneage died in hospital at Chemainus in 1946 at the age of 88. The hospital had thoughtfully provided a room for Eveline so she could help care for her brother in his last days. She moved to a nursing home in Victoria where she died in 1952 at 90. Both were cremated and buried on Thetis with a single headstone. In his will Major Heneage had left the property to the Anglican Church and so Camp Columbia, which has had thousands of visitors over the years, was born in 1947.

Reverend Thomas Robert Heneage, the youngest of the three brothers, was living in Vancouver when the eldest died in 1954. Thomas inherited the family estate and became Lord Heneage. (Alfred had been second in line.) Thomas was 76 at the time and remained in Vancouver. He was deaf and did not want to take his seat in the House of Lords.

Not all of Thetis's characters were English. One of the island's best-known latter-day residents was bearded "Cap Bardot," a French-born jack-of-all-trades who wore a jaunty old yachtsman's cap all year round. He lived on the island from 1940 until his death in 1976 at 94, with frequent trips to the pub at Chemainus. In his younger days he had served in the North-West Mounted Police on the prairies and later was a cook at the Reid Island cannery. Bardot was an artist, painting miniatures on oyster shells for the tourist trade in his later years.

KUPER ISLAND

Although neighbouring Kuper Island had two bands of Cowichan Indians—the Penelakut and the Lamalchi—it was not designated as a reserve when the first white settler arrived in 1870. William Conn pre-empted a section of land at Lamalchi Bay which he cleared and planted in fruit trees and grapes after building a log house.

After Conn's death his property was sold in 1880 to "The Company for Propagation of the Gospel in New England and Parts Adjacent in America," commonly known as the New England Company, an Anglican missionary society based in London. The site was picked by Reverend Robert James Roberts, who had first visited the coast two years before with his son Percy, 14, looking for a suitable mission site. They stayed in the Comox area while his wife Elizabeth "Lizzie" and three younger children remained in Ontario. Born in Ireland in 1831, Roberts had come to Canada in 1857 after missionary service in Australia and New Zealand, and had worked with the Six Nations Indians in Ontario.

Kuper was considered an ideal spot for a mission and residential school for young natives, because it was not close to any large Indian or white community. Roberts put up a building which served as church, school and community hall. It was built by Henry Bonsall with lumber towed from Thomas Askew's waterwheel sawmill at Chemainus on a raft built upon two large rowboats. The Roberts family moved to Kuper in January of 1882.

Elizabeth took over some of the teaching duties for her husband, helping the girls to learn sewing and putting up preserves, while the boys were taught farming by Reverend Roberts. There were about 22 pupils, although the Indian children went off with their parents fishing or working in canneries on the Fraser in the summer months.

The bridge between Kuper and Thetis had been built by that time, and for Roberts's Sunday service worshippers came by horse and buggy from Thetis and by boat from Chemainus, where there was as yet no Anglican church or resident clergyman. Roberts frequently went to Chemainus to conduct marriages, baptisms and burials.

Roberts was a frail but determined man. When Elizabeth went into labour on November 15, 1883, Roberts and Percy rowed to Ladysmith for the doctor but returned to find the baby, Victoria Mary Ellen, had been born with the help of an Indian woman. To a letter from the missionary society enquiring about his health, Roberts replied: "I suffer from epilepsy, flatulence, rheumatism, weakness of the heart and general debility, left hand and foot frequently almost numb from feeble circulation. Fainting fits come on almost every fortnight and sometimes more frequently." Toothaches were also a recurring problem, and all his ailments and "attacks" were du-

Reverend Robert J. Roberts. (COURTESY BC ARCHIVES)

tifully recorded in his diary. Despite his poor health, Roberts seldom flagged in his work before his retirement in 1902.[3]

But Roberts's condition and consequent gloom took a toll on his marriage. Lizzie was an energetic, cheerful woman who clearly longed for more fun than the Kuper mission provided. She made frequent visits to Chemainus to socialize with friends. On one occasion, when the family went to Nanaimo in their sloop, Lizzie decided to attend a charity masked ball. Roberts did not want her to go, but managed to persuade her only not to wear a mask. Her husband, who stayed on the boat, recorded sourly in his diary that she did not arrive back until five A.M. and slept until one P.M.

Roberts depended greatly on his son Percy, who from the age of 15 worked hard doing the physical tasks his father was unable to perform. He ran the boat, plowed the fields and performed an endless round of chores around the mission and family house. He too must have felt the strain, suffering like his father from debilitating headaches.

The Roberts had five children, three boys and two girls, Mary being the last and the only one born on Kuper. Edward died at the age of 27 on Kuper in 1888; Percy married Susan Holmes and settled on Kuper on the property which he purchased from the society, excluding the cemetery and mission building; Robert married Rose Prentice and moved to the north end of Salt Spring; Edith "Deena" married Arthur Nixon and settled on Thetis; and Mary married John Walcot and settled on Salt Spring. Roberts died in 1905 at the age of 74. Elizabeth moved to Victoria where she died in 1929.

In 1890 the Kuper Island School had been built on the west side of the island by the federal Department of Indian Affairs. The government paid the operating costs for the residential school but turned the administration over to the Roman Catholic Church. Although most of the teachers and support staff were not Catholics, the native students all took church instruction.

Having failed to fulfil his dream of building a residential school, Roberts was bitter about this arrangement. His diary recorded that on February 4, 1891, he was given a tour of the new school by the first principal. Father Gustav Donckele "brought me into one of the rooms which he has converted into a chapel, and fitted in the Romish fashion, which hardly seems right in a school maintained by public funds of the Dominion."[4]

Donckele, from the Victoria diocese and the first Catholic missionary in the Gulf Islands, served as principal with the assistance of the Sisters of St. Ann, who taught the girls for 17 years, until the school was turned over to the Montfort Fathers in 1906. The original building proved too small and in 1915 a four-storey brick building was opened. A large farm was operated by the school to teach the Indians farming, a favourite but futile endeavour of most B.C. coast missionaries; their charges never took to a settled agricultural way of life. Adult education was also part of the school program, however, and that was more successful.

By 1960 the school was reduced to grades one to five; the older pupils went to Chemainus. Fifteen years later the enrolment was down to 38, mostly children from broken homes, with 26 staff members. In June of 1975 the government closed the school down and island children commuted to Chemainus on the ferry each day. The big brick building stood empty for another decade before being knocked down.

Meanwhile, the 100-acre Lamalchi Bay property, first acquired by Conn and bought by the New England Company, lay abandoned for many years, surrounded by what was now an Indian reserve. In 1933 it was bought by Roy W. Ginn and his wife Audrey, who built it up into the Folded Hills Farm, specializing in raising cattle.

After her husband died, Audrey Ginn formed a business partnership with René Moeri, a diminutive Swiss-born cattle expert. Despite his size, René managed a herd of large Brown Swiss cattle, a breed akin to the French Charolais. To mark Canada's centennial in 1967 René cut the hay on a two-acre field and planted 17,000 flowers of 14 varieties in a pattern that spelled CANADA, ONE HUNDRED YEARS in 35-foot letters. A ten-province crest was also marked out, with each province represented by a different variety of flower. All were underlined and framed by other flowers. Planes buzzed over the island for days taking photographs of the colourful scene.

Indian children from the school had been called upon to provide music on special occasions since their band was founded by Father Donckele in 1890. In Canada's 1967 Centennial celebrations the

Students and teachers at the Kuper Island School. (COURTESY BC ARCHIVES)

Joe Silvey. (COURTESY BC ARCHIVES)

fife-and-drum band travelled to Expo 67 in Montreal. Funds were raised in Victoria to fly the band home when the fair was over. The 21 boys and ten girls may have been a big hit in Montreal in their spiffy red and white uniforms, but their parents wanted them back in a hurry so they could join the annual berry-picking jaunt to Washington state.

REID ISLAND

Lying between Thetis and Valdes islands is 240-acre Reid Island, which is associated mostly with three generations of the Silvey family. The original Joe Silvey arrived on the coast in 1849 on a Portuguese sailing ship, which he deserted off Point Roberts. With five of his countrymen he took part in the Fraser River and Cariboo gold rushes. Silvey moved next to Burrard Inlet where he opened a store in Gastown in 1865 and built the sloop *Morning Star* to trade with the Indians. While transporting herring to Porlier Pass for bait to catch dogfish, he saw Reid Island in 1872 and bought it for $2.60. Joe married an Indian woman from Sechelt and they had six sons and four daughters. After Joe died in 1902 his son Domingo took over the family home on the north hill of the island and made a living fishing and logging. Domingo died in 1941 and was buried on Reid near his father's grave.

There were six in Domingo's family, and his son Joseph Domingo Silvey, who was born on Reid in 1897, fished for 52 years and logged in the off-season on Galiano, Thetis, De Courcy and Valdes islands with horses and then steam donkeys. He remembered as a boy seeing a whale beached at Starvation Bay on Valdes that was 95 feet long and 14 feet wide. A dozen Japanese were cutting it up for oil.

Around 1908 two herring salteries operated by Japanese were started up on Reid, with as many as 150 men employed at each during the season. At one time there was also a cannery. A small school built by the Silveys, with eight to ten pupils, was run by the Catholics at first and then by the Department of Education before it was closed down.

Miners, Millstones
and The Brother XII

The most northerly of the southern group of Gulf Islands, Gabriola is due east of Nanaimo and separated at the south end by just 500 feet of water from Valdes. It is nine miles long and an average of 2 1/2 miles wide. Proximity to the "Hub City" has determined the island's character and development since the earliest days. The first settlers in the 1850s were coal miners looking for a place to farm. Gabriola, known as "the big island" in that area, was one of the most inviting spots.

A small Indian summer camp was situated at the south end facing Pylades Channel and De Courcy Island, but little else. There was some tall timber and enough pockets of good soil to hold promise of successful farming. Wolves were a threat to livestock around 1865, and the settlers lit pitch torches to frighten them off.

Some of the miners continued to work underground in the Nanaimo area and commute while building up their farms. The number of commuters has continued to increase and today they make up a large proportion of the population. An issue which now divides residents, about a third of whom are retirees, is that Gabriola might be linked to Vancouver Island by bridge and become a ferry terminal for a shorter strait crossing to the mainland. The idea of bridging the narrow gaps between adjacent Mudge Island and Vancouver Island, and Mudge and Gabriola, has been talked about for almost 60 years.

Gabriola has about 13,000 acres of gently undulating land and high sandstone cliffs. Its most photographed landmark is the spectacular "Galiano Gallery" (known also as "Malaspina Gallery,") on the north end at Descanso Bay. The curious open-sided tunnel runs 250 feet along the shoreline, 12 feet high with an average width of 17 feet. It was created by waves washing out a stratum of soft sandstone.

The first recorded white settlers were the Hoggan brothers, William and David, who arrived in the early 1850s from Glasgow by way of the Cariboo. They took up land around what became known as Hoggan's Lake on the west side, near Northumberland Channel. Their mother joined them in 1854 and an older brother, Alexander, followed soon after with his wife and six children. He had been working in the Cape Breton coal mines for about 15 years before deciding to move west.[1]

While William and David remained on Gabriola, Alexander went first to the Newcastle Island quarry near Nanaimo to earn money to support his family and then moved to the Wellington coal mine. He became a union leader and an organizer of the first strike at Wellington in 1877. When a sheriff was sent to evict his family from their company house, Hoggan put up a struggle and was arrested. He was convicted at the Victoria Assizes and served a three-month jail term, but went back to work in the mine when the strike was suppressed. Alexander's son James was killed in a mine explosion at Nanaimo in 1887.[2]

Another early Gabriola Scot was Alexander Shaw, who arrived in the late 1850s. He was the first telegraph operator on the island and the first postmaster, rowing to Nanaimo to pick up the mail. There was no school on the island until the 1870s and it was Shaw who gathered children together to teach them to read and write. With his two sons and young James Gray, the son of another settler, Shaw sailed to Victoria in a home-built boat to write a government examination for a teaching certificate. His son John later became principal of a school in Nanaimo, where his father had moved in 1888.

Robert Degnen, after whom Degnen Bay is named, was born in Ireland in 1832 and arrived on Vancouver Island in 1854. He became friendly with Robert Dunsmuir, who urged him to invest in his new coal-mine projects, but Degnen decided his first priority was owning a piece of land. He went to work for the Hudson's Bay Company to earn a salary, passing up the opportunity to become a wealthy man, for security.

Degnen met Robert Gray, another Irishman, at Wellington, where Gray was working in the mine. They became friends with the common goal of settling in the area. In 1862 Jane, an Indian girl living in Nanaimo, took them along when she went to visit her parents on the island. The two men liked what they saw and decided to settle there, tossing a coin to see who got what land at the south end.

The "Galiano Gallery" on Gabriola Island. (COURTESY BC ARCHIVES)

Degnen, who pre-empted 160 acres with good soil, also got the girl. He married Jane, the daughter of a Cowichan chief and a noted weaver. The Degnens had nine children, all born on the island, including sons Robert, Thomas and Frank. An innovator, Degnen built the first windmill on the Gulf Islands, to pump water to the house and fields. He also had the first wheeled conveyance on Gabriola. The wheels were sliced from the base of an old mast washed ashore from the wreckage of a large sailing ship; the iron bands which bound the mast stump were used as wheel rims.

Degnen started plowing with oxen, which he later replaced with horses. To supplement his food supply, he shot deer, grouse and pheasant, which were plentiful on the island in the early years. Expanding to 600 acres, Degnen ferried 37 ewes and a productive dairy cow to his property in a large dugout canoe that he owned jointly with Gray. The canoe could carry two tons fully loaded. Degnen specialized in sheep, but also had pigs, chickens and turkeys—the latter a favoured product of the island over the years—as well as an apple orchard. He tried peaches, but they failed.

Degnen used the canoe at first to carry his produce and that of his neighbours to market at Nanaimo, taking three hours to row over with 12-foot sweep oars. He carried potatoes, eggs, fruit, butter and cheese. As the freight business from the wharf he built in Degnen Bay continued to increase, Degnen replaced his big canoe with the steam launch *Patsy I*. She could carry 40 people as well as farm produce. Soon he was forced to lash a scow alongside to carry the loads. When the *Patsy I* was destroyed by fire, Degnen bought the *Patsy II*, a gas launch.

To supplement their farm income, both the Hoggans and Degnen got road-clearing contracts from the government, the Hoggans on the northeast end of the island and Degnen the south. There were no real settlements on the island for many years, only scattered farms. Gabriola tended to divide into two halves, north and south (actually northwest and southeast). There were post offices at either end and mostly wilderness in between. The majority of dairy farms were at the south, while beef cattle grazed at the other end.

Robert Gray also married an Indian woman and they had three children. Gray was an expert with the broad-axe and was in demand for barn-building. Before he died in 1908, Gray served briefly as keeper of the lighthouse at nearby Entrance Island, which helped guide ships into Nanaimo Harbour. A son, James, was postmaster from 1890 to 1895, and again from 1907 to 1930. James Gray married Jessie Aitken in 1896 and they had five children. Gray cleared and cultivated hundreds of acres in developing a cattle and sheep ranch and raising poultry.

Gray was followed at the lighthouse by M.G. Clark, another Gabriola resident. Clark's wife refused to live on the little rock, so she and the children stayed on the family's farm near Orlebar Point. To the displeasure of the lighthouse service, Clark spent considerable time there too, leaving the beacon in charge of assistants. When Clark was on the station, he often sent an assistant to work on the ranch; one was drowned in 1910 returning to the light from Gabriola, and Clark was later fired for dereliction of duty.[3]

Other early settlers in the southern interior of the island were Magnus Edgar, Richard Chappel and Thomas McGuffey. Edgar had come from the Shetlands, was hired first by the H.B.C. and then went to work in the Nanaimo mines in 1854. He pre-empted land on the southeast corner of Gabriola in 1862 and brought in the first yoke of oxen for plowing and stump clearing. Edgar's daughter Annie later married an Irishman, Daniel McConvey, who ran a logging operation using horses. He cut timber for the mines with Chinese workers.

Richard and Mary Chappel were an English couple who settled near the Edgars and the Shaws. Richard worked in the mines at Nanaimo before moving to the island in the 1860s. His son Joe went to work in the mines at the age of 13.[4]

Another family which left its name on Gabriola was that of John and Louisa Silva, who began on Mayne Island. Arriving on Gabriola in 1883 they took over a 133-acre property abandoned by Danish-born Henry Peterson on what became known as Silva Bay. This bay over the years has been the busiest anchorage on the island, sheltered by the Flat Top Islands. John built the *Corliss Queen* for fishing in local waters and off the mouth of the Fraser in the summer months. During hard times in the 1920s, John sold off parts of his property to bring in some money. He died at 92 in 1929, three years after Louisa.

Big families were common on the island. Henry Peterson and his Indian wife Jane had 12 children. The Peterson boys were regarded as hell-raisers, notorious for disrupting dances and other social events. Pit-lamping for deer was another of their pastimes. Eight of the boys served in the First World War, however.

John Silva had sold parcels of his land to Scotsman Alexander Law and his son Robert. Alex arrived on Gabriola in 1907 and Robert lived on the island from 1911 to 1963 after marrying Ruby Stenhouse. They had four children: Annie, Christian, Henry and Alison. Robert was active in community affairs on the island for more than 50 years, serving as a school trustee.

Another Scot, James Rollo, settled in 1874, his son John seven years later. The Rollos grew strawberries which were shipped to Nanaimo in 20-pound cedar crates. John later started a freight business and brought the first car to Gabriola on a scow in 1912.

Pioneer settler Abraham Crocker married Louise Silva, daughter of John and Louisa, and they had 15 children. Crocker spearheaded a drive to build a Catholic church and persuaded John Silva to donate the land. Daniel McConvey and his son William used horses to take logs for the building off the property, and James Gray and Thomas Degnen also took part in the project. The church was opened in 1912, with services conducted once a month by priests from Kuper Island, and the sturdy little building still stands at Silva Bay.[5]

William Coats settled on 80 acres at the north end in 1912 and grew cauliflowers. He opened a store in 1928 which he ran for the next 16 years. A versatile man, Coats was also a bricklayer, and built chimneys and ovens for the Brother XII complex on De Courcy Island. Coats had the first school bus on Gabriola and also purchased some of Brother XII's goods to sell in his store when the commune broke up, including a thousand jars of preserves, sacks of sugar, farm machinery and garden implements.

Gabriola's first school was opened at the south end in 1873, near the present community hall grounds, after a school district was incorporated. Trustees were Tom McGuffey, Magnus Edgar and John

Kemp, who donated two acres of land. The first teacher was an American, E.L. Seneker, who had 16 students.

North-end residents complained it was too far for their children to walk and began petitioning Victoria for a new school in their area. Mrs. Alex Hoggan took a leading role in the campaign. Action was taken in 1883 when the island was divided in two for school purposes, and two trustees were named for the north end. The petitioners had asked for $500 but only $200 was forthcoming, plus $30 for furnishings. The school opened in a primitive building on October 11, 1883. The first teacher was Miss J.A. Scott, followed the next year by Margaret J. Sweet. The school was closed in 1889 because there were not enough students, but the following year a new school was built at the south end. The two school districts were amalgamated in 1936.

As on most of the islands, sandstone once provided Gabriola with a valuable industry—the quarrying of building blocks and the cutting of huge grindstones for paper mills. The quarry was started about 1887 in the southeast corner of Descanso Bay. In 1900 it was taken over by the Vancouver Granite Company. The old Victoria Post Office at Government and Humboldt streets is built of Gabriola stone.

The millstone operation began in 1932, also at Descanso Bay. Used at Ocean Falls and Powell River mills and shipped as far away as Scandinavia, the huge spinning wheels turned logs into pulpy mush. About a thousand were shipped from the island, worth about $600 each. Most were exported in the years 1932-36 by the J.A. and C.H. McDonald Stone Company.

Cut out by a special saw, each millstone weighed about five tons: they were three to five feet in diameter and two to four feet thick. Ten-inch-diameter holes were cut in the centre for the drive shafts. (The cores were used as corner foundations for many of Gabriola's early houses.) The millstones were lifted by huge tongs and trimmed on a giant lathe. Two 50-ton derricks were installed, one at the quarry and the other at the wharf where barges were loaded. James Rollo carried the stones from the quarry to the wharf on his one-ton, single-axle truck.

Another major industry on the island was a brickyard that went into operation about 1895 and operated for almost 50 years. A number of Chinese workers were employed at the plant, located at the bottom of "Big Hill," known today as "Brickyard Hill." Electricity for the drying kilns was introduced in 1914. The bricks were carried on horse carts down the hill to Descanso Bay to be loaded on scows bound for Nanaimo and Vancouver.

The brickyard was located at False Narrows across from Mudge Island. The property had been purchased from a pioneer, William Nairn Shaw, who later donated land for a community hall at the south end. A number of Chinese workmen lived in bunkhouses nearby. By 1917 a total of 3,500,000 bricks had been shipped. In 1937 the plant employed 28 men. In its last year of operation in 1945 it shipped 1,800,000 bricks. The Dominion Brick and Shale Company also operated a shale mine for tiles at Descanso Bay and used crushed shale in the manufacture of firebricks.

Tobacco had always been grown in a small way on Gabriola and in 1911 some hundred pounds of "Nanaimo Mixture" were shipped out by a local group. Today the crop of choice for smoking is more likely to be marijuana.

The most notable churchman associated with Gabriola, Reverend George William Taylor, spent just a short time on the island. Taylor was born in Derby, England, in 1854 and trained as a mining engineer, but was interested in all the natural sciences. After he moved to Victoria in 1879, Taylor was persuaded by Bishop George Hills that the mines were dangerous places to work and that he should enter the Anglican ministry. He was ordained by Hills in 1884 and married Elizabeth Williams the following year. She was the headmistress of the Girls Central School and organist at the cathedral. His first posting was a parish at Wellington, ministering to the coal miners and their families. At times he went down into the tunnels to comfort men injured in cave-ins or explosions.

While carrying on his church work, Reverend Taylor made a study of the local marine life and built up an outstanding collection of moths and butterflies. After three children had been born, tragedy struck in 1895 when Elizabeth died ten days after their fourth child was stillborn.

Taylor considered going back to England, but Sam Robins, su-

Reverend George W. Taylor. (COURTESY BC ARCHIVES)

perintendent of the New Vancouver Coal Company of Wellington, a rival of the Dunsmuir empire, was so impressed by his work with the miners that he persuaded the minister to stay by giving him 100 acres of waterfront property on Gabriola. Taylor moved to the island in 1896 and lived for two years in a cottage with his two sons and a daughter at what is now known as Gabriola Sands Park on Taylor Bay, just north of Descanso Bay. As well as continuing his parish work around Nanaimo, he preached in the Descanso schoolhouse and walked ten miles once a month to Degnen Bay and back to hold services in the schoolhouse there.

In recognition of his scientific work, Taylor was made a Fellow of the Royal Society of Canada. At the time of his death in 1912 he was the only Fellow west of Winnipeg. A paper that Taylor presented to the society was instrumental in persuading the Dominion government to establish the marine biological station at Departure Bay, and in 1908 he retired from the ministry to become its first curator. He bought ten acres nearby, but was stricken by a severe heart attack in 1910 and died two years later.

By 1906 Gabriola had 200 permanent residents and 25 miles of roads to replace the early network of narrow paths and rutted wagon trails. A number of Vancouver residents put up summer cottages during the 1920s and '30s. The population has grown steadily and today the island has 2,800 residents, second only to Salt Spring among the Gulf Islands.

VALDES ISLAND

Lying to the southwest of Gabriola, Valdes Island is a slender and shorter extension of Galiano, from which it is separated by Porlier Pass. Valdes is heavily wooded, almost uninhabited; its shoreline is mostly steep and uninviting. A third of the island is Indian reserve, including the southern end where there used to be two native fishing camps at either end of the pass.

An early resident of Valdes was Captain Baldwin Arden Wake, an Englishman who had retired from the Royal Navy. In England Wake had been involved in organizing an industrial training school, which gave him some qualification for teaching. He lived on the north end of the island and rowed across Gabriola Passage into Degnen Bay each day to teach at the south-end school. A crusty disciplinarian, Wake was disliked by his students and their parents, who prevailed upon the trustees to have him ousted in 1879. They succeeded, but only after a nasty war of words. The school closed for the next two years when enrolment fell below ten, but reopened in 1881 under Alex Shaw.

Wake died in 1880, apparently drowned while returning in his sloop to Valdes from Nanaimo. The boat was found washed ashore on Thetis Island with its mast snapped. Six boxes of personal effects, including silver plate, clothing and books were aboard, having been shipped to Nanaimo from England. Some of the boxes were found, emptied, on a nearby beach and Wake's son found some of the silver plate buried in the sand. It was speculated that Wake had been attacked by robbers, or the goods were taken after they were washed ashore. His body was never found.

After her husband's death, Mrs. Wake moved to Esquimalt with their two daughters and mixed in Victoria society, becoming friendly with the Crease family; she died in 1894. The son, Baldwin, stayed on Valdes and worked as a telegrapher until his death in 1906. His widow, Amelia, remained on the island, also working as a telegrapher, for 64 years until her death in Nanaimo in 1946 at the age of 87. The family lived at Wake's Cove, a rendezvous on Valdes for the Royal Vancouver Yacht Club.

In 1895 the residents of Valdes got together to put up a log building to serve as a school. Kate V. Smith was the first teacher and there were 18 pupils. A school district was formed in 1910, but the school closed permanently in 1936 when the depression forced most of the settlers to leave the island.

Both Valdes and De Courcy, the latter owned in 1889 by William Flewett, who was plagued by sheep rustlers, are associated with the the cult of the notorious Brother XII, now the subject of renewed interest by historians. He began as plain Edward Arthur Wilson, born in Birmingham, England, in 1878. Little is known of his early life, but Wilson is said to have worked for an express company in Victoria about 1910, and another report had him working in Nanaimo as the "lamp man" for the Dunsmuir coal mine. There he worked above ground, filling and repairing the oil lamps, with plenty of time for reading.

After travels during the 1920s in California, Tahiti, France and Italy, Wilson resurfaced in this area as The Brother XII and founder of the Aquarian Foundation, which at its peak had 8,000 members around the world. It was a period when theosophy and the occult were in vogue, and Wilson had learned much of the teaching and jargon of these beliefs. With a number of supporters from England he settled first in 1927 at Cedar, six miles south of Nanaimo, where 200 building lots were purchased. The colony prospered and the foundation acquired 400 acres on Valdes where Wilson built a house. Later, he acquired the largest of the De Courcy Islands, directly east of Cedar. Wilson often went to Gabriola to pick up his mail, which included cheques from adherents abroad.

There was an attempt to create communal settlements on both islands, but as is often the case with such enterprises, beset by internal feuds, it soon foundered in a storm of accusations, lawsuits and courtroom confrontations. Wilson returned to Europe around 1930 and apparently died in Switzerland in 1934, although that too is a matter of controversy. Mary Connally, one of the women Wilson is alleged to have bilked of large sums of money, was still listed as the owner of De Courcy in 1939 but was unable to keep up the taxes there or on her property on Valdes, on which she owed $425. She eventually moved to California.[6]

One of Abraham and Louise Crocker's daughters, Grace, who married Frank Gibson, spent some time on Valdes during the depression. Frank was out of work and when the couple found an abandoned house on the island in 1939, without doors or windows, they moved in. The Gibsons then went to the Indian Agent at Nanaimo and leased the house, which stood on reserve land, for ten dollars a year. They plowed the land and planted fruit trees and vegetables. Later they went to work on De Courcy Island for Mrs. Connally, who paid them ten dollars a month each for working on her garden.

Alone among the Gulf Islands, there are fewer residents on Valdes today than there were a century ago. It has no ferry service and no tourists except boaters. There are no services and only a handful of determined get-away-from-it-all summer cottage dwellers.

Feuds, Wife-Swapping and an Opera House

L asqueti has a history unlike the other Gulf Islands. Its relative isolation in the middle of the strait, half way between the Sechelt Peninsula on the mainland and the Qualicum area of Vancouver Island, brought a different kind of settler and way of life. The pace is slow and there are few amenities. At first glance it would appear to be the rustic paradise many Gulf Islanders think they want.

But appearances are deceptive. Instead of a homogeneous population bound together by common problems, Lasqueti more often than not has had feuding and squabbling unmatched on the other islands. It's a John Steinbeck or Erskine Caldwell kind of place: there has been no lack of offbeat characters for a novel.

The distinction of being the first white settler on Lasqueti is generally given to George Tranfield. He was a butcher with his own meat market in Nanaimo when he decided in 1860 to run sheep in the False Bay area at the northwest end of the island. It was known as Foul Bay at the time, but the name was later changed to reflect the fact that it was a deceptive haven for boats—a westerly gale can whip in suddenly. Close behind Tranfield was William Jeffreys, who jumped ship from an English sailing vessel and settled at Tucker Bay on the north side.

There were a few more pre-emptions in the following two decades, but little development. The next settler of note, in 1882, was Hugh Henry "Harry" Higgins, a former British soldier who had been stationed on San Juan Island during the boundary dispute. Higgins built a two-room house of upright logs with a sandstone fireplace on seven acres of waterfront sheep-grazing land at the north end facing the Finnerty Islands. In 1889 he married 14-year-old Mary Ann Jeffreys, daughter of William Jeffreys. A year later Mary Ann delivered their first baby, a girl, by herself.

Higgins gained some notoriety in 1895 when he swapped wives with another early resident, William Rous. Young Mary Ann Higgins became Mary Ann Rous and Margaret "Maggie" Rous, 53, became Maggie Higgins. The foursome stayed on the island for a time, before Rous and Mary Ann moved to Pender Island. After Maggie Higgins died in 1917, Harry was married again, to Hazel Goodale of Nanaimo.[1]

In 1891 John Stapleton Grey Pemberton discovered the island. "A footloose Englishman who was circumnavigating the world, [he] passed by Lasqueti, fell in love with a spectacular sunset and so bought the entire northwestern peninsula," an area of more than 1,200 acres. After buying up a number of other properties, Pemberton returned to England, leaving his land in the care of Harry Higgins, who built a house on the property. The size of Pemberton's holdings, added to the 2,000 acres owned in the south by an English consortium, McLaughlin Estates, blocked settlement of the island for years.[2]

In the 1890s a rough livestock fence was erected from Tucker Bay to Richardson Bay, dividing the island in half, with Pemberton to the north and the McLaughlin land on the south. In 1911 a retired R.C.M.P. officer, John Norrish, bought the McLaughlin property; Norrish's son Dawson and his wife Alice later took it over.

In 1898 the Sisters Lighthouse was built on a bare little rock northwest of Lasqueti. The first keeper lasted less than a year. The next man to try was Harry Higgins. At the end of his first winter on the rock Maggie Higgins left "because of the clamour of the fog bell every thirty seconds, which cracked plaster throughout the interior." Higgins soldiered on until February of 1901 when he rejoined Maggie on Lasqueti.[3]

Higgins resettled at Boat Cove, started an apple orchard, helped organize the Lasqueti Farmers' Institute in 1912, and became road foreman. He was also involved in the establishment of a co-op store at Tucker Bay in 1919. Higgins and his third wife, Hazel, moved to the Pemberton house across from the Finnerty Islands, where they lived out the rest of their days.

In 1902 the Kurtzhal brothers, Rudolph, Otto and Alex, arrived from Denmark. Their countrymen Nels and Tom Christiansen already had an orchard at the south end of the island and the Kurtzhals bought 480 acres in that area. They sold pork and mutton in Nanaimo, which they delivered by rowing and sailing across the windswept strait. When the worst weather forced them to seek shelter, the return trip could take as long as two weeks. Alex Kurtzhal worked at various times at the mines on nearby Texada Island.

One of the aspects of life on a small island that either appeals or repels is that there are few secrets. Everybody seems to know everybody else's business. Lasqueti, except for its communal period in the 1960s, has always been a more private place. Few of the scattered cabins are within sight of one another, tucked away in the bush or in tiny coves. For this reason it has attracted a large number of eccentrics, recluses and worse.

Among the latter just after the turn of the century were bachelor Bill Julian and Henry Wagner and his wife, settlers apparently leading quiet lives together on the island. Only later did it turn out that their means of livelihood was robbery—making raids on Vancouver Island settlements and high-tailing it back to Lasqueti. The two men were eventually caught holed up in an isolated cabin at Davis Bay after a robbery and murder at Union Bay. Julian was jailed for the crime and Wagner was hanged at Nanaimo on August 28, 1913.

The year 1913 also marked a happier event—the arrival of Charles Williams and his wife Della, an energetic woman who had come from Medicine Hat. Williams was a go-getter destined to play a key role in Lasqueti's affairs for the next half century. The couple had no children.

Starting out as logger, fisherman and beachcomber, Williams opened a store at False Bay which Della operated, as well as a hotel and marine ways. He brought the first car, which was used to deliver mail and groceries, to the island. Elected a school trustee in 1918, Williams held that post for 38 years. He was a justice of the peace from 1926 to 1968 and coroner from 1950 to 1963.

But Williams is remembered more for his exploits on behalf of the False Bay area in its feud with Tucker Bay for island dominance. Tucker Bay took the lead briefly around 1913 when the co-op and first school were built there. False Bay followed with its own school in 1915, a shack furnished with wooden boxes from the cannery. An upright box served as a desk, and a box on its side was a seat. Williams moved into action to boost attendance at the new school. He went to Tucker Bay and offered a logger, who had a large family, a job and a house at False Bay. When the logger accepted, the Tucker Bay school's population was reduced to below the provincial minimum and it was forced to close. Desks were removed and the building was used as a community hall until 1932, when it was able to re-open as a school.

Tucker Bay had made another bid for island leadership in 1913 when a wharf was built to enable large vessels to unload settlers, freight and mail from Vancouver. Mail had previously come by small boat from Nanaimo or from Qualicum, where a fire was built on the beach as a signal that there were letters to be picked up.

Now that the steamships *Cowichan* and *Comox* were providing a more regular, reliable service, the island's first post office was built at Tucker Bay, but that little settlement's triumph was short-lived. In 1923 the *Cowichan* hit a rock approaching the bay. After an underwater survey, Union Steamships decided the entrance was too dangerous and the service was cancelled. Mail and supplies now came by small boat from Pender Harbour on the mainland once a week.

False Bay, led by the indefatigable Charles Williams, was poised to take advantage of its new opportunity. In 1923 he bought fish-cannery buildings which had been erected at False Bay in 1915. Prior to 1915, fishermen had sold their catches to packers from Nanaimo. The False Bay Fishing & Canning Company, which built the cannery, was associated with the San Juan Canning Company of Friday Harbor on San Juan Island. Fish were delivered to the False Bay cannery from surrounding areas, and bunkhouses were built for Chinese workers. As well as salmon, the plant began canning clams and herring during the war. A brief spurt of prosperity was enjoyed by Lasqueti, but when the bottom fell out of the world tinned-salmon market in 1918 because of a glut, the cannery was forced to close.

In 1923, Williams turned the cannery into a fish-reduction plant, drawing more settlers in need of a paying job to the area. Dogfish and salmon offal were processed for fish meal and fertilizer until 1926, when fire destroyed the plant.

In the meantime, a new wharf had been built at False Bay and, amid much bitterness, the post office was moved there from Tucker Bay. The hostility led to a wrestling match over some mail bags when the transfer was first made.

Union Steamships resumed service to Lasqueti in 1927 at the False Bay wharf and at floats off the centre and south end. The population in the early 1920s was 140. By 1926 it had dropped to a mere 11, with another 25 living on fishboats. Then, as the depression settled in, the population jumped to more than 300 as new homesteaders arrived, hoping to make a living off the land. That was not easy.

The lack of arable soil and water has been a continuing problem on the island. Hydro-electric power has never arrived, and only private generators are in use. There have also been problems associated with the island's "open range" policy for livestock. Cattle, horses, goats, sheep and fowl have grazed freely along the roadsides, chewing up wildflowers and encouraging rustlers.

Some settlers came to Lasqueti with innovative ideas. Paul Lambert arrived in 1919 on a boat named the *Black Fox*. He planned to produce prime fox furs by shipping the animals north in the winters to thicken their coats, but the logistics and cost of transport doomed the scheme from the start. Lambert also failed with muskrat and nutria. Then he brought in edible frogs which he mailed to some of the rich and famous in Hollywood, hoping to garner some publicity. More failure for Lambert, but his frogs thrived, spreading into the island's five lakes.

Most of the island's deer population was killed off during those hungry years. Salmon runs were poor so the fishermen went for ling cod for food instead. When most of the island's young men left for the war in 1939, life became even more discouraging.

Not for Charles Williams, however. He managed to get a limited phone service for Lasqueti in 1927 after persuading the Liberal government that it would be a vote-getter. A cable was brought over from Sechelt, but there were only three shared phones on the island for many years. Service had expanded to 22 homes on a party line when the system was taken over by the B.C. Telephone Company in the late 1960s and the cable laid from Qualicum.

False Bay had become the focal point of the island by then, largely through Williams's efforts. His wife played an active role too, especially in the operation of the family store. She was called upon for extra duty in July of 1948 when the steamship *Cardena* ran on the rocks in fog at the entrance to False Bay. Lifeboats managed to get everyone ashore safely and Della Williams took care of more than a hundred passengers, packing them into every corner of the Williams's house and store. The ship was later refloated and made it back to Vancouver under her own steam for drydock repairs.[4]

Lasqueti once laid claim to some of the best stands of red cedar on the coast. In 1898 the Rat Portage Timber Company of Vancouver began logging this treasure near Boat Cove. A steam donkey engine was placed on a long jetty extending into the cove from the eastern shore. The skid road leading to the jetty later became part of the government road. Some of the trees were so big that the company was unable to get them out with the equipment of that time. Giant rotting logs and stumps are still visible today.

Rat Portage ceased operations in 1911 and for a number of years the islanders continued logging on a limited scale. A small group of Japanese families at Mud Bay, a section of False Bay, formed a logging company using horses, but left the island in 1928. Tractors were used to haul logs in the 1930s. It was not until the 1950s, and the use of trucks, that logging thrived.

Little has changed on Lasqueti over the years; it is still one of the least developed of the Gulf Islands. There is no car ferry and autos for use on the island's few roads must be barged over from French Creek on Vancouver Island. There are no school classes beyond Grade Seven. Tension between the young dropouts who descended on the island in the 1960s and the old-timers has dissipated in recent years as islanders joined together to fight off development.

TEXADA ISLAND

In contrast to the other Gulf Islands, Texada is thought of in terms of its industry rather than its farms, resorts and salubrious climate, although the weather is equally fine. And unlike the others in this book, Texada's connections have been with the mainland, with Powell River and Vancouver, rather than Vancouver Island. Even its immediate neighbour, Lasqueti, is tied to Vancouver Island by its ferry service.

Texada is large: thirty miles long and an average of five miles wide. Its harsh and abrupt shoreline contributes to the feeling of alienation. It is not a pastoral island like the others. There is only a small amount of arable land, around Gillies Bay and in small pockets in the central valleys. They tell of one determined gardener who carried soil laboriously to his little plot by the bucket load.

Blubber Bay at the northern tip of the island was briefly the site of a whaling operation, but that activity was short-lived in the Strait of Georgia. Texada old-timers could remember, however, when whale fat and livers were boiled in huge black iron pots on the beach.[5]

More than any of the other islands, Texada has had a boom-and-bust economy, tied to the fortunes of mining. The man who set the mineral rush in motion was Harry Trim, generally agreed to have been the island's first settler. Whaler, fisherman, logger and prospector, Trim lived at Blubber Bay. On a prospecting junket in 1871 he found outcroppings of iron ore on the west side at Welcome Bay, three miles northwest of Gillies Bay.

That discovery led to the new province's first major political scandal, involving former premier Amor De Cosmos and other prominent figures. They were accused of using their positions to secretly pre-empt mineral properties on the island. De Cosmos, who had resigned as premier after a short term to become a Member of Parliament in Ottawa, insisted he was interested only in the province getting its own iron-ore mine. He was not a shareholder but admitted he had tried to sell the mine property to English investors for a fee. The sale never came off.

The commissioner, Chief Justice Matthew Begbie, concluded there were suspicious circumstances surrounding the wheeling and dealing, but that allegations of corruption had not been proven. De Cosmos, Begbie said, had failed to discriminate between his duties as a member of the government and his rights as an individual. That ended the "Texada Scandal," but not the questionable activities of politicians in the handling of provincial resources, an on-going theme in B.C. history.

The controversy over Texada's iron-ore deposits came to the attention of some U.S. businessmen who were planning a steel mill at Port Townsend, when it became the western terminus of the north-

Mining operation at Marble Bay. (COURTESY BC ARCHIVES)

ern transcontinental railroad. The railway never got farther than Seattle, but the American-owned Puget Sound Iron Company bought the Texada mine in 1875 and it was worked intermittently over the next 30 years by that firm or lessees. Ore was shipped to a smelter at Tacoma starting in 1883. "Although the Texada iron operation of this period was in the nature of a small quarry rather than a regular mine, it can be said that it was the first base-metal mine on the B.C. coast and the forerunner of a major industry."[6]

There was a new flurry of excitement around 1880 when gold and copper were found on the island. A number of properties were opened up, including the Little Billie gold mine, and the first wave of fortune hunters descended. A tent camp sprang up on the northeast shore where the twin towns of Texada City and Van Anda were later to arise.

Within the next few years, seven mines were operating in the Van Anda area, with such exotic names as the Gold Bug, Golden Slipper, Black Prince and Copper Queen. American entrepreneurs were at the centre of the activity. Ed Blewett of Tacoma, backed by New York financier Harry Whitney Treat, formed the Van Anda Copper and Gold Company. In 1898 they opened a small smelter which operated for the next 12 years near the wharf in Van Anda Bay. Another American active in Texada mining ventures was James Raper, who started the Cornell Mine, also in 1898.

One of the best-known miners around the turn of the century was Ed Russ, who had worked at camps in the U.S. southwest before arriving at Marble Bay. Later he settled in a cedar-shake cabin near Gillies Bay and went prospecting. With a long white beard and walking stick, he was a familiar sight on Texada hillsides.

By 1900 the population had risen to 450, and in the heady days of the next decade would climb as high as 3,000. Most of the activity was around Marble Bay, which had earlier been noted for a quarry that produced high-grade marble for the old Hotel Vancouver and other buildings in Vancouver.

Texada City had blossomed first and was so sure of its future that it built an ostentatious opera house containing a great banquet hall. Like most "opera houses" in the boondocks, the entertainment fell far short of the Met and was usually closer to burlesque. Old-timers remembered for years the grand ball that was held there around the turn of the century to raise money for the Boer War. The opera house building was later turned into a hospital.

When the Van Anda Copper and Gold Company laid out a townsite with 300 lots for sale, Texada City was merged into the new centre of Van Anda. One of the more flamboyant methods used to sell the lots was the chance to win a 26-room hotel which had cost $5,000 to build, a healthy sum in those days. The lots were priced from $75 to $150, but the Texada real-estate bubble burst before they were all sold. The lottery was called off, the hotel prize was never awarded, and the building stood empty for years.

There were already three hotels flourishing at the time, however, each with its own crowded saloon. Van Anda also boasted three general stores, a hospital, a drug store, a jail and a newspaper. The paper was the *Coast Miner*, published bi-monthly by Jack Lawson of Vancouver, a former school teacher. The well-known newspaperman and B.C. historian Bruce "Pinky" McKelvie cut his journalistic teeth on the *Miner* as a printer's devil. McKelvie's father was a mechanic in charge of installing the furnace at the smelter.

Texada has always been vulnerable to fires. Summers are often hot, dry and windy. In 1910 a brush fire ran out of control and burned down seven commercial buildings in the new town. Two years later the rebuilt stores were levelled by another blaze, and there was yet another disastrous fire in 1917. The buildings were all of wood frame construction and water was scarce.

Texada's prosperity lasted until the end of the First World War. The closure of the Marble Bay gold mine in 1919 marked the end of an era on the island. There were lean times for the next two decades as mining virtually came to a halt. Grant Brothers of Comox had opened a small sawmill on the island in the early 1900s, but logging did not become a major industry there until 1945.

One of the island's best-known characters in the early 1900s, Walter "Steamboat Bob" Piddock, was associated with the early sawmill, carrying lumber on his vessel *Wood Nymph* to logging camps in the area. Piddock also towed booms and scows, and did a little beachcombing. An Englishman who never lost his accent, he liked to dance and would carry groups of dancers on the *Wood Nymph* to wherever there was a party. Piddock and his little steamer were eventually beached by a stringent new Boiler Inspection Act.

Most of the early homesteaders settled in the centre of the island toward the south end, often on a lakeshore. The records of these small farms are scanty. Their owners are remembered only as "Hobo Tom," who raised pigs, and other similar recluses. The McElroy family lived on one of the larger farms three miles north of Gillies Bay which was known as "the settlement." Whatever produce could be wrested from the scraggy ground was consumed or bartered locally. Almost all the dwellings were built of logs retrieved from land-clearing operations.

The first school on the island, which opened in 1898, was a room in the log house of Mr. and Mrs. Whitney Treat. As enrolment grew it was moved to an old mess hall beside the noisy sawmill, which made teacher Emily Raper's work even more demanding. On Sundays, when the mill was idle, the school was used as a church. For many years Texada had only a number of one-room schools scattered about the island.

The only relatively stable industry over the years was limestone quarrying. It kept the island going between mining booms. The first wood-burning kiln to extract lime from the stone was built at Blubber Bay in 1887, but large-scale quarrying by the Pacific Lime Company did not begin until 1907. At one time four quarries were in operation, each exporting 60,000 to 130,000 tons of limestone annually. Much of this production was shipped to the B.C. Cement Company plant at Bamberton on Saanich Inlet, north of Victoria. Chinese and Japanese labourers were hired as quarry workers. The old iron-ore smelter, which had been idle for 35 years, was revived as a rock-crushing plant for the limestone industry.

In 1952 iron-ore mining was resumed, with different methods and a new market. Huge open pits were carved out of the landscape and the ore was loaded, after going through a flotation mill, onto freighters bound for Japan. This operation lasted for 25 years until the high-grade ore was mined out and the mine shut down.

Texada had two cottage industries over the years of a dissimilar nature. One was the gathering of glossy blueberry branches which were exported for use as background sprays for floral arrangements. More exciting—and lucrative for a time—was moonshining.

Abandoned mine shafts and lonely coves at the south end proved ideal spots for whisky stills. This Texada brew was sold from the Sechelt Peninsula north to Alaska. Most of the operators were said to have deliberately kept out of the Vancouver market to avoid strife with the big-city bootleggers.

At least one distiller who tried to expand his market was nabbed by Customs agents. The agents had engaged pilots from the Jericho air base to help them crack the illegal trade. "The Customs Department had learned that a certain scow would depart in tow from a berth in False Creek and return within the day with suspected consignments of illicit brew. . . . One day it was observed that the outgoing empty scow had on board a white horse, and that the horse was not aboard when the scow returned." The pilot, with a Customs agent aboard, eventually spotted the horse at a secluded Texada cove. "Inspection of the cove revealed a large, thriving, industrial still, ingeniously concealed from view from the air by branches of trees that were pulled together over it by ropes and pulleys. The enterprising lawbreaker was convicted."[7]

As on many of the other Gulf Islands, one of Texada's most colourful and best-remembered residents was a clergyman. Reverend George C.F. Pringle spent less than a decade on the island, but they were nine memorable years. After mission work in the Klondike—he was ordained at St. Andrew's Church in Dawson City—and in the trenches in the First World War where he was known as "the sourdough pastor," Pringle was named in 1920 to take over the Presbyterian Loggers' Mission. Based in Van Anda, he served 6,000 loggers in 75 camps along 200 miles of coastline in the mission boat *Sky Pilot*, a 40-foot vessel with a 30-hp engine. Included in his routine were four visits a year to Lasqueti to hold church services attended by 50 people, or one-third of the island's population.

Although less rugged physically and temperamentally than his elder brother John, also a minister in the Yukon during the gold-rush days and later Moderator of the General Assembly of the Presbyterian Church in Canada, George got on well with the hard-bitten

Reverend George C.F. Pringle. (COURTESY BC ARCHIVES)

loggers. He had patience, energy and a dynamic personality, with a gift for humour, story-telling and making friends.

Pringle pitched in to help fight forest fires, visited sick men in their bunkhouses and took the injured or seriously ill to hospital on the *Sky Pilot*. His experiences made him an early proponent of state medical care. In 1930 Pringle was appointed pastor of Centennial United Church in Victoria. He continued to keep in touch with Texada Islanders and other upcoast friends until his death in 1949, at 76.

A famed kerosene lantern which was hung on the porch of the Pringles' house on the hill above Van Anda was used as a beacon by Union Steamships vessels and the *Sky Pilot* returning from mission calls. A second lantern was hung on the port corner of the Van Anda wharf by the postmaster, and ships took their bearings from the two lights.

Despite these precautions, disaster struck in the early hours of January 7, 1913, when the Union Steamships' *Cheslakee* sank at the Van Anda wharf. She had left Van Anda earlier for Powell River with 89 passengers. While crossing Malaspina Strait she was caught in a sudden squall and began listing after some cargo shifted. Big seas washed into the open freight doors. She got back to Van Anda but heeled over while trying to tie up to the dock; six passengers and a crew member died. The vessel was later salvaged and went back into service as the *Cheakamus* for another 30 years. An inquiry into the sinking criticized the addition of a superstructure heavier than the designer had allowed for. It was a criticism applied to a number of coastal vessels which ran into trouble in that era.[8]

Centralization was impossible on Texada because of the island's size, small population and lack of roads. Many of the early settlers' log cabins were built in isolated spots along the shore, and they used boats and trails to get about. As on Lasqueti, tourism and service industries have played only a small role in the island's history compared to others in the strait.

The Union Steamships' Cheslakee *at the Van Anda dock.* (COURTESY BC ARCHIVES)

A Cycling Parson, Orcadians and Bull Whackers

More than any other of the Gulf Islands linked by proximity, Denman and Hornby are truly a pair. There's really only one way to get to Hornby—catch a ferry from Vancouver Island to Denman, drive across Denman, and then take a second, short ferry ride to Hornby. Denman itself has the shortest ferry trip of all the Gulf Islands from Vancouver Island. It is just two miles across Baynes Sound from Buckley Bay. Lambert Channel, separating Denman from Hornby, is only one mile wide.

Originally heavily timbered, Denman is 13 miles long and has an average width of about 2 1/2 miles. Its highest point is 400 feet, and there are a number of large marshes and two lakes. There is good farm land on the west side. The island had no resident Indians, but the Puntledge tribe from Comox had summer camps for hunting, fishing and clamming.[1]

The Baynes Sound coal-mine development in the early 1860s on

Vancouver Island had brought to the Buckley Bay area a hotel, store and sawmill, and the promise of jobs and markets for produce, but it foundered in 1869. The victims of the closure looked to Denman as a place to settle, and there was a sudden scramble for land on the island. It would be another decade before the big Cumberland coal mine was opened up, creating new jobs and markets.

Settlement flourished in the 1870s with the arrival of a number of British immigrants who had gone first to New Brunswick and become acquainted there. Many were from the Orkney Islands—so many, in fact, that Denman was once known by the locals as "New Orkney Island." It has been estimated that Orcadians and their descendants comprised one-third of Denman's population in 1927. Most of the pioneers travelled from Vancouver via Comox on the steamship *Maude*. Supplies came twice a month on the boat from Nanaimo and were unloaded onto rafts or rowboats before a wharf was built on the west side.

In 1874 Peter Berry and his partner William Robb had squatted on land in the Madigan marsh area at the centre of the island. Robb killed and butchered a bull every two weeks just before boat-day, when the meat could be delivered to Comox or Cumberland. Alex McMillan and Jim McCoy went to the west side. McCoy later sold his 320-acre property to McMillan, who started a prize-winning Jersey herd. The following year machinist David Pickles and his brother Abraham arrived. James Henderson and George Edwards settled on the east side in 1876, the same year the Piercy clan arrived from New Brunswick.

Matthew and Agnes Piercy, from Northumberland, England, had emigrated to New Brunswick about 1840. They moved west in 1874, arriving in Comox in the fall with their two youngest daughters and four unmarried sons, as well as son Tom and his wife Jane and their four young children. Four other married daughters in this extended family remained in New Brunswick. (At a reunion in 1979 in Comox, 832 members of the family turned up.)

After spending their first winter—an unusually severe one—with their cousins Mr. and Mrs. George Gartley in Comox, sons Tom and John Piercy pre-empted land on the west side of Denman. Tom, the eldest son, became one of the island's most active residents. He was Denman's first justice of the peace and served as road foreman. His daughter Margaret in 1878 was the first white girl born on the island and son Harvey the first boy in 1880. Tom and Jane planted a thousand fruit trees, mostly apples. The Piercy home was known as "The Ranch," a gathering place for residents and visitors.

Among the influx of new settlers in 1876 were the five McFarlan brothers from the Orkneys by way of New Brunswick—Walter, Charles, George, John and Jim. The McFarlans, who acquired land on the east side, had the first horse and wagon on Denman. In 1883 twins Walter and Charles built the first ship on the island, a schooner to run to Nanaimo with produce and return with provisions. The sails were designed and handsewn by George Heatherbell of Hornby.

Before the advent of the schooner, the settlers had taken their surplus butter and eggs by rowboat to Union Bay and bought staples at the store there, occasionally travelling farther north to Courtenay.

Tom and Jane Piercy, with ten of their 11 children. (COURTESY BC ARCHIVES)

The McFarlan brothers, joined by three brothers-in-law, built a rough sawmill and installed an overshot power wheel to grind grain. In 1896 the McFarlan families moved to the Hawaiian Islands, although some second-generation members returned to Denman in later years. Mrs. Catherine McFarlan, mother of the five brothers, died in Hawaii close to her 100th birthday.[2]

The first settlers learned quickly to be self-sufficient. After choosing meadows or bottom land easy to clear, they cut shakes for their cabin and barn roofs from the abundant cedars. The cleared trees were also used to make rough furniture, small boats and dragsleds. Sheepskins were used as mats, blankets and chair coverings. The sheep wool was carded, spun and woven into clothing. The pioneers learned to tan deer and cattle hides, and cure ham and bacon. Fat was saved to make soap, and mutton tallow was used to make candles and grease machinery.[3]

In 1876 brothers John and Charles McCutcheon also arrived from New Brunswick with their families in Buckley Bay, where Charles became the timekeeper for a small mining operation. Moving over to Denman, the McCutcheons began pressing with Tom Piercy and boatbuilder Alby Graham for a school. The settlers got together in 1878 and rafted lumber from Vancouver Island to put up the first schoolhouse in the central district. It opened with 14 children—six Piercys, five Grahams and three McCutcheons. John McCutcheon was the first schoolmaster. There were no desks, just benches around the walls, and the students did more reading and oral work than writing.

By 1882 there were 23 pupils, but the school was forced to close the next year when Tom Piercy moved back to Comox with his family to be nearer to his relatives, drastically reducing the enrolment. The school stayed shut for five years, then reopened when Piercy returned (with the addition of two more children) following rumours that the Buckley Bay mines would operate again. The report proved to be wrong, but the bigger Cumberland mine (it was called Union then) began operation shortly afterward, and Piercy was ready. From his 240-acre farm he sent butter, eggs, fruit, meat and vegetables to the new coal mine. When another daughter was born in

The Graham homestead, ca *1888, John Graham at left, Albert at right.*
(COURTESY BC ARCHIVES)

1890 he put an addition on his house to accommodate the ten of his 11 children still at home.[4]

The year 1878 marked the arrival of Robert Taylor "Bob" Swan, who became "the grand old man of Denman." Swan had gone from Scotland to New Brunswick with his parents in 1850 as a boy of three. He learned the blacksmith's trade there and lost an eye in a smithy. Swan moved to the west coast in 1874 after marrying Charlotte Warden. Working first on the Cariboo Road and then logging around Harrison Lake, Swan moved to Vancouver Island to work on construction of a railway from the Baynes Sound mine to Buckley Bay. When that scheme failed he worked as a logger and building contractor in the Comox area.

Swan moved to Denman and bought 160 acres on the west side, where he built a house, and sent for his wife and children in New Brunswick. In all the Swans had ten children—six sons and four daughters. One son died in infancy. Swan farmed on Denman and did some logging on Vancouver Island; he was also the postmaster on Denman for 28 years. He and his son Sandy ran a little ferry, the

Goey, to the Courtenay River wharf, where they had to wait for high tide to land.

Swan donated land for a Methodist church. The first services by a visiting minister had been held in 1879 in the Swan house. In 1888, with pioneers Alex McMillan, Tom Piercy and Jack Piket, Swan helped put up the building which became known as "the United Church on the Hill," on a rise near the main road-crossing on the island. The first service was conducted on December 26, 1888, by Reverend Walter W. Baer, with 48 in the congregation. The church later switched to the Presbyterian denomination before becoming a United Church, and is still standing.

One of the ministers, Reverend W. Kidd, also held services on Hornby and at Union Bay around 1910. He used to leave his boarding place at the Piercy ranch early Sunday morning, cycle across Denman, put his bike in a small boat, and row across to Hornby. There he would cycle two miles to the schoolhouse for the service, returning to Denman in the same manner for an afternoon service. After supper Kidd rowed to Union Bay for an evening service.

For many years after the Denman church was completed, Swan made coffins for the community with left-over lumber. His coffins were noted for their craftsmanship, not the run-of-the-mill, straight-angled box but enlarged and rounded at one end to fit the shoulders.

A second farm came into Swan's hands when an early settler, W.S. "Bob" Yates, died. Yates had no heirs and left his property to Swan because Swan had been helpful to him. Swan moved to the Yates property after his original house burned down in 1895. A warm-hearted man, Swan made pets of his farm animals and deer. Among his many talents was that of water-diviner, a skill much in demand on the Gulf Islands. Swan lived till 1940, dying at the age of 93.

Another arrival from New Brunswick with Swan in 1878 was William M. Dingwall, who had been postmaster at Buckley Bay for a year before buying land on the west side of the island. Dingwall was later elected to the legislature from the Comox riding, which included Denman. He was successful in getting the first wharf built on the island in 1886. Dingwall was a jolly man despite poor health; he was only 38 when he died of pneumonia in 1889, not long after his general store at the Comox wharf failed because of over-extended credit.[5]

Tom Pickard moved to Denman in 1878 and acquired property near Metcalfe Bay. He opened the island's first store at Barcroft Flats in 1886. His relatives from Nottingham, England, the John Pikets, arrived soon afterward and Pickard paddled a raft out to take them off the steamer. The Pikets raised six children on the island, one of whom was born in Nanaimo after a canoe journey from Denman. Later, the Pikets built the first hotel in Cumberland and an inn on the road between the mining town and Courtenay. Their married son Tom moved back to Denman about 1912 onto property left to him by Peter Berry.

In 1885 Judge Henry Crease of Victoria bought land from Tom and Walter Piercy which he leased for a proposed hotel. When the settlers made it clear they were strongly opposed to a licensed liquor outlet on the island, the lease-holder backed out, and Crease was left with the property. The foundation timbers and framing for six rooms on the second floor had been completed, but Bob and Sandy Swan dismantled the structure and salvaged most of the lumber.

George David Beadnell first saw Denman as a young man of 20 on a hunting trip while visiting an uncle in Cumberland. Beadnell boarded with the Pikets and wrote in glowing terms of the island to his mother and father and sister Maud at home in Warwick, England. They soon joined him, and his father, a doctor, bought 200 acres from pioneer logger Bob Yates on the east side facing Hornby, in what became known as the Beadnell's Creek area. Dr. Beadnell resumed his medical practice on Denman and Hornby, and is remembered for bringing the first piano to Denman. His nephew Harry Beadnell later bought the adjoining John McCutcheon property, and a trail was cut through the woods between the two houses. Harry was a fisheries inspector in the Comox area for 21 years until his retirement in 1935.

The Beadnells called the estate "Fillongley," after their ancestral home in Wales, and turned it into a private park with rockeries and trellises, a bowling green and a tennis court. The work was started by Dr. Beadnell and his wife, who moved to Comox in 1902, and was carried on by George and his wife Amy. Amy Bastin had come

Dr. and Mrs. George Beadnell at Fillongley. (COURTESY BC AR-CHIVES)

from England as governess for the four children of Maud and her husband, Horace Smith of Comox. Amy was an ardent gardener and planted roses, rhododendrons and assorted flower beds. After she died in 1932 George kept adding to the grounds, installing a sundial, rustic furniture, bird houses, and a bridge over the lily pond. Favourite trees were given names such as "Darby and Joan," "Beauty," and "Daddy." When Beadnell died in 1958, aged 89, he bequeathed the estate to the provincial government for a public park.

In 1890 a lighthouse was completed on Yellow Rock, a two-acre pillar off the southeast tip of Denman that was renamed Chrome Island in 1940. The original name came from its annual spring covering of yellow daisies. The island is also noted for a remarkable variety of Indian rock carvings, or petroglyphs. Some were lost in blasting the site for the lighthouse.

Tom Piercy was the first lightkeeper, starting on New Year's Day, 1891. Conditions were primitive, rainwater being collected in cisterns in the basement. Piercy had his family with him on the rock, including ten children. One of the boys, eight-year-old Harvey, was playing with a blasting cap left behind by the construction workers when it exploded, tearing off the end of his thumb and injuring two fingers. Tom bandaged the hand and rowed him across to Denman. The keeper was not allowed to leave his station and the rest of the family was away visiting, so Piercy was forced to leave the boy with directions to Dr. Beadnell's house, six miles away by trail. The doctor treated the wounds and took Harvey to hospital at Cumberland.[6]

The lighthouse had been built at the demand of the coal-mining companies for a beacon at the entrance to Baynes Sound. It did not save the 220-foot freighter *Alpha*, however, which sank after hitting Yellow Rock at 6:45 P.M. in a southeast gale and snowstorm on December 15, 1900. Nine men were drowned, including Captain F.H. Yorke. Twenty-six reached safety by clinging to a line one of them fixed to the rock. The survivors were fed and sheltered by keeper William McDonagh, who had succeeded Piercy.

The *Alpha* was bound for Union Bay to load her bunkers with 320 tons of coal for a voyage to Japan. She was carrying 630 tons of salted dog salmon, which washed up on the beaches and was salvaged by the islanders for fertilizer.

Like most of the Gulf Islands, Denman had a sandstone quarry. It was started in 1908 by Sam Dumaresq and other investors who bought 25 acres from Robert Swan. Dumaresq later built a large home for his wife and six children, who moved over from Vancouver.

By 1910 up to 30 men were employed in the quarry operation. The derrick which loaded the heavy building blocks on scows was one of the largest in the province. A wide-gauge railway carried the stone to the wharf. The stone was used for the old Normal School and the main post office in Vancouver, Victoria High School, and the interior of the Parliament Buildings. It was discovered, however, that the stone became streaky when exposed to weather and the quarry closed down in 1915. The stone had been prized by chandlers because it was particularly good for holystoning the decks of ships.

After the quarry closed Dumaresq went into logging, the island's major industry for many years. It had begun with George Edwards and Joe Rodello driving teams of oxen on Beadnell's Creek. Starting in 1876, they sold logs to the Piddock sawmill on the Courtenay River. Rodello, a colourful character who had been a soldier with Garibaldi in his native Italy, had started in the area by purchasing land at Comox from pioneer James Robb on both sides of the road at the head of the wharf. He built a store and restaurant on the east side and the Elk Hotel on the west before moving to Denman. Rodello had also been a constable and tax collector.

It was Orkney Islander Bill Baikie and his three sons who expanded logging in the area. Baikie had arrived at Christmas of 1888 at the urging of Reverend Baer. He had met the clergyman while working on a farm in Ontario. Baer came out first and then wrote back to Baikie. Baikie went originally to a sawmill at Cumberland and then to Alex McMillan's ranch as a farmhand for $250 a year, plus board and washing. After acquiring 40 acres of his own on the east side, this go-getting young redhead was soon a force on the island. He became a fire-ranger, road foreman and active Liberal, which may have helped him acquire the first two positions.

Baikie married Tom Piercy's daughter Selena in 1898. Their first child, Winnifred (later Mrs. Tom Isbister, a Denman historian) was born in 1900. Wallace arrived two years later and five other children followed. The youngest daughter was born in 1917 after Dr. Meadows had arrived to take up practice on the island. Before he came, midwife Jane Piercy had delivered most of Denman's babies.

Bill Baikie's father, William, an Orkney fisherman, came to Denman about 1890 and helped his son clear the land for his ranch. The son also recruited a number of other settlers from his birthplace. In 1895 Tom and Jack Chalmers, who lived in the same Orkney village as the Baikies, arrived on Denman and bought the property of Charles McFarlan. On a visit to the Orkneys in 1907 Baikie brought back his niece, Annie Corrigal, and five young men—John Robertson, Bill Isbister, Tommy Scott, John Baikie and Bill Wood. His sister, Mrs. James Corrigal, followed with her husband a year later.

As well as logging, Bill Baikie ran a farm and orchard. He and Tom Piercy took prizes for their apples at competitions in Vancouver. Piercy had 800 trees which filled 3,500 boxes in 1912. Farm produce from the island was shown at the Comox Fall Fair in the early days, but after George Dalziel organized the Denman Island Farmers' Institute in 1915, the island began holding its own agricultural fair in the community hall. That lasted only until 1925, however, because most of the men by then were logging rather than farming. One holdout was Marcus Isbister, who exported 15,000 Christmas trees in 1948, as well as a hundred tons of potatoes and turnips. Denman turnips were prized for their sweet crispness. They were first grown by Japanese farmers around Lacon Marsh at the south end.

Like many boys of his age, Wallace Baikie left school at 14 to work in a logging camp as a whistle punk. In log-rolling competitions, at which they won many trophies, the Baikie brothers, Wallace, Harper and Jack, were known as "The Birling Baikies." They worked for others until 1934 when, out of a job in the depths of the depression, the brothers formed a "gypo" outfit, Baikie Brothers Logging Company. They borrowed a team of horses from their father and with inherited determination, expanded the firm over the next 30 years into a flourishing timber empire.

With his partners Jack Scott and Tom and Jack Chalmers, Bill Baikie began logging with horses in the winter months. When spring came they went back to farming. To the transplanted New Brunswickers, the west coast trees seemed immense. "Such timber called for heroic logging. Being easterners they set to work with the methods they knew, with ropes and oxen and poll axes. Being lumbermen, and therefore inventive, they adapted their ways to the giant trees and mountainous terrain. Where four oxen might serve in the east, 10 or 12 were needed here... they fashioned wooden skid roads from poles, like trackless railways, and greased them with oil to give the bull teams a fighting chance."[7]

The skid poles were nine feet long and placed nine feet apart, peeled and dug into the roadway to stop them from rolling. A gentle, consistent downhill slope was the ideal. The skids would be slightly flattened where the logs were to slide. The key to the operation was the man in charge of the bulls—the bull whacker, bull puncher or bull skinner. All the animals had names and were talked to and sworn at. When words failed to move the 1,600-pound animals, the bull skinner used a slim pole with a barb on the end to prod them in the rump.

Each pair of animals was held side by side with a carved wooden yoke fitted over the backs of their necks. "A chain or cable is hooked on to each yoke as it goes down the line, so when each animal moves ahead, he is actually pushing rather than pulling." The yokes of five or six pairs were shackled to a line running back to the logs being pulled, a string of half a dozen making up a "turn." At the bottom of the skid road the logs were jacked over a "roll way" of poles into the water.[8]

The skid logs were greased with foul-smelling dogfish oil, applied by Japanese or youths starting out to become loggers. The dogfish were speared along the shoreline at night when they followed spawning smelt into the beach. A big fire was built in the morning to render the livers into oil, which was stored in wooden barrels.

Oxen were replaced by horse teams about the turn of the century. Although they could not pull as much weight as the bulls, horses were easier to train and faster-moving. Four Piercy brothers built a

Skid-road logging, ca *1904. l. to r. Howard Fairbairn, Jack Chalmers, William Baikie, Ray Chalmers.* (COURTESY BC ARCHIVES)

skid road down to Isbister Beach in 1908, using a four-horse team. Other loggers employing horses in the early days on Denman were Bill Day and his brothers, and Jack Scott from Hornby. Day also logged on Hornby before moving to Campbell River, where he lived past the century mark.

Jack Martin logged above the Beadnells and built a chute to dump logs into the sea; Frank Stewart had an eight-horse operation at Henry Bay; and Howard McFarlan, the son of John McFarlan, brought the first steam donkey to Denman in 1906 at Henry Bay. He used a six-horse team to move the logs from the skid road to the beach.

Logging on Denman ran its course through oxen, horses, a railway and, after the Second World War, trucks. In 1915 Chester Yapp supervised the construction of a rail line for the Squamish Logging Company which ran from the Pickles' ranch to Randall's Spit. Just before the war the Henry Bay Railroad Company, operating a gas-powered locomotive, logged Canadian Collieries land at the north end of the island. This operation was able to take out some of the biggest trees which earlier, smaller outfits had been unable to handle.

Henry Bay was also the site of a commercial clamshell operation for a number of years. Clamshell deposits six feet deep were found at the head of the bay. Some believe they were deposited by Indians over the centuries; others think the shells were washed into the bay by tide and waves. In one year 3,000 tons of crushed shell were shipped by barge to New Westminister, where it was sacked for agricultural lime.

In 1916 the islanders, led by Sandy Swan and Bill Baikie, installed their own telephone system with 30 customers. Shares in the co-op cost $61, but could be paid off by digging postholes and raising poles. The hand-cranked telephones cost an additional $25. Each household had its own ring, using a combination of five. One long ring was a call for emergency help, such as the volunteer firefighters. The phone was also used to warn of the presence on the island of the game warden, who was trying to halt the pit-lamping of deer, a common practice. In 1926 the system was connected to Vancouver Island and the mainland by the B.C. Telephone Company. Service expanded slowly, however, as the permanent population of the island dropped during the depression years, starting in 1929 from a high of 350 to 200 in 1959, when it began to increase again.

There were a few Japanese-Canadians on Denman at the turn of the century, but none remained when the Pacific war started in 1941. Frank Uyehara, the eldest son of a Salt Spring family, logged on Denman for a time. Five Kawamura brothers bought farm land near Lacon Marsh in the 1890s to raise sheep and cattle, and grow vegetables for the Cumberland market. The Kawamuras also enlarged a tidal pool into a commercial holding tank for ling cod. Their farm was sold to Reginald Lacon in 1910.

l. to r. William Baikie, Robert Swan, George McFarlan, 1929.
(COURTESY BC ARCHIVES)

HORNBY ISLAND

Although Hornby was called the "Outer Island" by the Indians and Denman the "Inner Island," it was Hornby that was settled first. The land on Hornby was more open, less densely forested than its sister island. Development was still slow, however. Settlement began in the 1870s, but the population had reached only 50 by the turn of the century, and more than a third were children. Land under cultivation was a mere 400 acres on 12 farms. Of the original pre-emptors, mostly English, only three still owned land; some properties had simply been abandoned.

George Ford and Henry Horatio Maude, friends from Devon, had arrived in the Comox Valley in the summer of 1862 after trying their luck in the Cariboo gold rush. Ford is believed to have moved to Hornby in 1869 and Maude soon after. They were an odd pair. Ford was robust and gregarious; Maude sickly and reclusive. When there was a dispute about almost anything, they were invariably on opposite sides. In common, both men had Indian wives, were in their early 30s when they arrived, although Maude seemed much older, and apparently had incomes from England. The Maudes had one child, a step-daughter, while the Fords had nine. A private school funded mostly by Ford was built in 1880, with eight of his children at one time making up the total enrolment. The first public school was opened in March of 1892 and is still standing at a new location on Sollans Road.[9]

By 1885 the two men between them owned almost half of Hornby. Ford had 1,800 acres of mostly open land at the southwest end and Maude 1,400 acres, including both Tribune and Whaling Station bays. They built a trail between the two properties. Both had chosen natural pasture areas that required little clearing; they ran cattle and planted orchards and vegetables, and Maude grew tobacco. Maude had a 45-foot dugout canoe that required four oxen to haul it in and out of the sea at Tribune Bay, where he also kept horses and played polo on the beach. Ford's sons cut cordwood for steamships which loaded at their wharf in Ford Cove. Later they married Indian women and went into fishing. Ford and Maude both died relatively young, Maude in 1888 at 55, and Ford ten years later at about 65. Maude left his land to his nephew, David L. Herbert, who lived there only briefly.[10]

The Ford children gradually disposed of the property left to them, except Martha, who married James Strachan. He had arrived from Aberdeen in 1880. The Strachans had nine children and settled on Marsh Farm in what became known as Strachan Valley. It remained in the family for generations. It was one of the most productive farms on Hornby, exporting vegetables, beef and dairy products. The Strachans worked for a time as lightkeepers on Yellow Rock, where their daughter Jessie was born. Jim Strachan lived to the age of 90 and Martha was 89 when she died in 1967.

Over the years dairy herds replaced Shorthorn beef cattle on both Denman and Hornby. A creamery opened in Courtenay in 1901, which processed island produce delivered by motorboat.

Wallace Pevey pre-empted 120 acres of forested land near Grassy Point some time in the 1870s. He logged with oxen and towed small booms around to Ford Cove. Loggers at that time had only long pike poles for moving logs in the water and Pevey saw the need for a shorter pole with a hinged hook at the end to roll them into position on land or water. "And so the first pevey (peavey) was born in his welding shop." The tool was advertised in the *Lumberman's Gazette* in 1878 and was soon in great demand. Pevey patented his invention and left the island a rich man.[11]

Logging continued on a small scale until about 1910 when operations were expanded, including the construction of a primitive railroad on log tracks with wide flange wheels. After a decade, most of the commercial timber had been taken and the Hornby loggers moved to Vancouver Island sites. Baikie Brothers returned in the spring of 1936, however, to log two small claims on the east side of Hornby. They had a flat-bed truck loaded with a cook stove, beds, blankets, tents and supplies. Wallace took his wife Myra and a baby along, as well as a cook, Anna Macartney. Caesar Scott, Tom Shaw, Jack Piket and a few others camped in Gaston DePape's hayfield for six months. The company bought an old Bay Elder logging truck at Deep Bay and built a dumping wharf at Tribune Bay. In the fall they moved to the north end of Denman, finishing up there in 1938.

George Howe was a successful butcher and businessman in Comox and Union Bay who pre-empted land on Hornby in 1878. He let his beef cattle run loose on the island, leaving his farm in the hands of a caretaker. A cousin, John Howe, settled on Hornby in the 1880s.

The next early settler of note was George Heatherbell. He began with a small holding about 1876 at Phipps Point, where he built up a farm and orchard. In 1884 he married Matilda Ann Graham of

Robert Swan, at the age of 80. (COURTESY BC ARCHIVES)

Denman. Heatherbell had earlier pre-empted what was to become the Fillongley Park property on Denman, but did not improve it. After expanding to about 400 acres on Hornby, Heatherbell built an imposing home he called "Maplehurst" for his wife and eight children. Robert Swan had come over from Denman to help brace the huge beams in the seven-room house. The lumber had been shipped from Vancouver.

Heatherbell had been joined for a time by his older brother William, who had gone with him on a Klondike expedition. William's wife was killed in the Point Ellice Bridge collapse in Victoria in 1896 and he left Hornby not long afterwards.

George Heatherbell was on friendly terms with the Indians, spoke Chinook and traded with them. Frustrated eventually by the lack of ferry service, roads and communications, he sold Maplehurst and the land in 1902 to Tom Smith, and went to Victoria to work for the government as a horticulturist. Later he moved to Tasmania and died in New Zealand in 1943 at 91.

Smith continued to run the property as a farm with his wife Margaret and served as justice of the peace. He had changed his name from Lea-Smith to just plain Smith because, he said, an Englishman had enough problems in Canada without a double-barrelled name.

Smith had spent his English inheritance and had to work hard to keep the farm going in the 1920s and '30s. He had sheep and chickens, grew hay and oats, and was the first to bring Aberdeen Angus cattle to the island. When times improved he hired farmhands and lived the life of a gentleman. He enjoyed playing the violin and driving his Model-T Ford. Smith worked the farm for 39 years until his death in 1941. Maplehurst burned down a few months later while it was being rented, and another house was built on the site. Mrs. Smith died in the Campbell River hospital at 105.

John Scott had pre-empted 160 acres in the centre of the island in 1888 and farmed with oxen. He raised seven sons who became expert boatmen and fishermen. Two of them, Jack and Washington, moved over to Denman, where Washington married a niece of the Rogers Chocolate family, who had a holiday place there.

Jack Scott was a logger, blacksmith and boatbuilder who also worked as a labourer for Dave Pickles and other farmers on Denman. In 1899, he married Mary Miller, an Orkney Islander he met while she was visiting Bill Baikie and the other Orkney families on the island. Another brother, Caesar, logged and farmed on Hornby and opened the Sea Breeze resort. He was also one of the first oyster farmers on Denman. Jack Scott built up his herd of oxen to ten and used them in the 1890s to become the first logger on Hornby. He also transported the mail across Lambert Channel from Denman to Hornby, first by dugout canoe and then by rowboat.

Robert Solan, a former railway engineer, settled on the north end near Grassy Point about 1880. He was a lonely bachelor who decided to advertise for a wife. Following up one of the replies, he travelled to Chicago and married a woman said to have weighed close to 300 pounds. On his return Solan found that the buggy seat on his wagon could not support both of them, so he walked alongside leading the horse. Later he switched to an ox because he said it was faster than the horse, but it may have been its ability to pull heavier loads that influenced him.

One of Hornby's most interesting settlers was Walter Gordon, who had come from New Brunswick with his mother in 1902 as caretaker-renter for one of the Ford properties. He was described as "a tall, bewhiskered, raw-boned, friendly middle-aged man [with] a jolly Ho Ho Ho laugh."[12]

Gordon followed McDonagh as keeper of the Yellow Rock lighthouse for five years. In an effort to avoid the regular rowing trips across to the end of Denman for water and firewood, he built a crude aerial tramway over the quarter-mile stretch of water with a basket hanging from a taut rope. Unfortunately, the line broke on his second trip across and he was dumped into the sea. A neighbour who was fishing nearby, Fred Scott, plucked Gordon from the water.

An artist, Gordon dabbled ineffectually at farming, letting his cattle run wild. On one memorable occasion Gordon wanted to get a bull across to Denman. He tied it to a rock at low tide and waited for the incoming tide to float the animal so that he could make it swim across. Clever idea, but the bull circled the rock several times, shortening the rope. When the tide came in Gordon swam out to the animal with a large butcher knife between his teeth. After struggling unsuccessfully to untie the rope, he decided to cut it. The bull headed immediately for the beach and disappeared into the bush.

Gordon also tried a unique way of shipping his pigs to the butcher in Cumberland—on the hoof. He built a pen, open at the bottom, with a horse hooked on to the front end. "As the pen was moved ahead the pigs were to run along to keep from getting run over. This procedure worked fine for a mile or so until they arrived at the top of the mountain with dense brush on both sides of the narrow road. The pigs by this time were tired and decided to have a sit-down strike. The result was the open bottom pen bumped right over the pile of pigs and another of his bright schemes had gone awry."[13]

A life-long bachelor who always wore a ragged English jacket, Gordon was a big man with a deep voice who liked to sing and play the flute. When he wanted to get from his farm to Vancouver Island he would land his little boat on the east side of Denman and walk five miles across to Alex McMillan's place with a handful of four-inch spikes in his pocket and a hammer on his belt. There he would assemble a raft on the spit to continue his journey across Baynes

Sound to Union Bay. Once he paddled over astride a flat cedar log.

Gordon managed to sign up for service in the First World War in the Forestry Unit even though he was close to 60. He was about to be sent back from England after his age was discovered when he managed to get work in an ammunition plant. He returned to Hornby after the war and died of pneumonia in hospital at Comox, aged 85. He was buried beside his mother in the Denman cemetery.

There were a number of Chinese on Hornby at the turn of the century, most of them working for the enterprising Yick Shing, who bought the old George Ford house and farm. They grew cabbage and celery for the Nanaimo market, transporting it in Yick's boat with a hired seaman. At the same time, Yick was importing sacks and sacks of rice via Union Bay for his labourers. At least, that's what he said it was for. In fact, Yick was making rice whisky, which he smuggled in the boxes of vegetables bound for Nanaimo. His still was found hidden under a hay mower in a barn on his property near Heron Rocks. The law eventually caught up with Yick and he was sentenced to jail for three years.

The ingenious Yick was one jump ahead of his captors, however. He later told Tom Smith that because "all Chinese were considered to look alike," he alternated his sentence with an accommodating cousin. Visitors were allowed into the cells every two or three weeks and Yick and his cousin were able to split the sentence by simply switching identities, exchanging their clothing while the guard was out of sight.[14]

The Sydney Slade family bought land at Whaling Station Bay in 1914. The sandy beach there had long been a fishing and camping place for the Comox Indians. The Slades worked closely with the natives, who helped build their log house. Whaling Station Bay had been used in the 1800s by the B.C. Whaling Company as one of its bases in the Strait of Georgia. It was given up in 1872 when the firm went bankrupt because there were not enough whales left in the strait to support the industry. The 100-acre property, including a wharf, frame building and cooper's shop, was auctioned off. The station had been in operation only during 1871.

More people arrived on Hornby in the 1920s, but others left during the depression in the following decade. Residents scrabbled food from their farms and the sea. Some fruits and vegetables, mostly tomatoes, were sold to a cannery at Comox during its four-year existence in the mid-1930s. The plant was forced to close when store-bought canned goods became a luxury during the hard times of the depression. Settlers who fished with their rowboats delivered salmon to the cannery at Deep Bay on Vancouver Island. A barter economy thrived during these lean years.

Social life centred around the Women's and Farmers' Institutes, which had been transplanted from England. The Farmers' Institute sponsored lectures, maintained the cemetery and bought blasting powder in bulk for its members. The women's group organized social events, sponsored concerts and lace-making and weaving demonstrations, and put up jars of berry jellies and jams for Britain during the war. Dances, public meetings and political debates were held in the one-room schoolhouse. The Hornby Community Hall, built by volunteer labour, opened in 1928.

The first church was not opened until 1950, on property donated by the Savoie family. The Roman Catholic Holy Cross Church was blessed on May 19 of that year by Bishop Hill of Victoria. Up to that time the Catholics held services in private homes. Other denominations used the schoolhouse and community hall, with ministers visiting from Vancouver Island.

A co-op store was started in the mid-1950s. When business was slow, manager John Richards piled merchandise in his car and circled the island, peddling his goods door-to-door.

The character of Hornby has been changing dramatically in recent years. The population has shot up to 1,200 permanent residents and more than double that number in summer. Real estate prices have escalated accordingly and many of the older residents are fearful of the consequences of the new influx of wealth. The island's sandy beaches, warm-water swimming and spectacular sandstone shoreline are a magnet for holidayers. Denman, on the other hand, has retained more of its early lifestyle. Although it too has attracted retirees, there are still productive farms on the island and with a population just a little more than half of that on Hornby, the pace is less hectic.

Rowboats, Sidewheelers
and Ferries

When the first Gulf Island settlers went from Victoria to Salt
Spring in 1859, their only means of getting there was to hire
one of the local trading schooners. These sailing vessels carried their
belongings to the beach or landing area nearest the property they
were pre-empting. The *Kate*, *Wanderer* and *Black Diamond*, which
were also involved in the fur-sealing trade, continued to serve those
pioneers until steamships began stopping at the islands.

Most of the first homes were cabins built from readily available
logs or rough-cut lumber, but some pioneers shipped lumber and
bricks from Victoria by schooner, tug and barge, or canoe. The first
cattle were brought over that way, loaded at Victoria with block and
tackle and pushed overboard close inshore at the islands so they
could swim to the beach.

Once settled on an island, the pioneers' first priority was to acquire their own boats. Most began by buying or trading goods for

an Indian dugout canoe. Others fashioned crude rowboats or skiffs. As a few skilled settlers arrived with better tools, and finished lumber became more available, the vessels became more ambitious. Boats were then bought or bartered for.

Most common were sturdy clinker-built (overlapping half-inch planking), 12- to 16-foot workboats with two sets of oars, a mast and gaff spar and rough sail. Many had ribs every six inches for strength, and a four-inch keel.

There were few sailing craft in the first decades with full keels to allow tacking, so the islanders had to hope for following winds, or resort to pulling on the oars. If winds were light they put up the sail *and* rowed. The distances that strong and skilled rowers were able to cover in a few hours are astonishing to the modern sailor. Although it was some years before published tide tables were common, the settlers learned by experience how to take advantage of the local currents. Drownings were frequent, however, in the cold and dangerous waters.

Over the years these small craft assumed every shape and size—

Sloop Dawendeena, *belonging to Reverend R. Roberts.* (COURTESY BC ARCHIVES)

flat-bottomed, double-ended, boxy or sleek. Some settlers acquired larger craft such as 27-foot whaleboats with five oars. Alexander Brackett of Pender travelled in a 16-foot, double-ended Columbia River fishing boat. Trips across the strait to the mouth of the Fraser for supplies became routine for some settlers.

The inventive Canon Paddon of Mayne had a wondrous contraption: a rowboat-sized craft with sidewheels that he rotated by hand with two cranks. Rowing might have been easier, but he enjoyed visiting his parishioners in this unique way.

Small gasoline engines were installed before the turn of the century and distances became less daunting with the addition of this power. Many people still preferred quiet, and the aroma of the sea, to noisy motors and exhaust fumes, however. As the recreational seamen began acquiring comfortable yachts, regattas became popular events on the islands.

The first commercial steamship to serve the islands on a semi-regular basis was the American-owned *Fideliter*. She began calling at Vesuvius on Salt Spring in 1864, but that service lasted only two or three years. Next were the Victoria-based sidewheelers *Amelia* and *Isabel* which stopped at a number of Gulf Island points on their way to and from Nanaimo. The *Isabel* had been launched in Victoria in 1866 as a tug for timber entrepreneur Captain Edward Stamp, while the *Amelia* was built in San Francisco and worked the Sacramento River before she was sold and moved north. These two vessels provided the first real ferry service along the east coast of Vancouver Island and the Gulf Islands.

Not everyone was happy with the service. Vesuvius was too far away for farmers at the south end of Salt Spring who needed to get their produce to market. They employed a variety of craft—sloops, schooners and canoes—to carry meat, vegetables, fruit, tobacco and cedar shakes to Victoria. Indians were also hired to transport the goods in their big canoes.

Regular ferry service to Salt Spring Island was slow in coming. There was little development in Ganges even by 1890, and the steamers called irregularly at Fernwood, Fulford Harbour, Burgoyne Bay, Beaver Point and Vesuvius, site of the Bittancourt store.

Agitation for better service, including daily mail delivery, was led by the Reverend Edward Wilson.

By 1905 Ganges had blossomed into a busy settlement and Reverend Wilson noted in his diary: "It is no unusual thing now to see as many as twenty or more farmers' waggons, buggies and other equipment assembled under the trees at Ganges wharf when the steamboat comes in. Rather different to ten years ago when there might be seen tethered to the same tree half a dozen or so saddle ponies and perhaps two or three ox teams."[1]

The scene on boat-day was much the same on the other islands. On Mayne "the farmers came to the village with their cans of cream, the Japanese with their trucks loaded with cases of tomatoes to be shipped to the mainland. Don Vigurs was on the wharf with his truck ready to receive his shipment of groceries coming on the *Princess Mary* from Vancouver." When there was a lot of freight the boat would be docked for half an hour or more, allowing visits on the pier with travellers to the other islands.[2]

At the centre of the pier activity was the ship's purser. He was the man who dealt with special requests by island residents, bought and sold items on commission, and handled the mail. One of the best known was Harry Austin, who would take verbal requests at dockside and have the items on the next trip. He seldom forgot an order. John Wilson, purser on the *Maude* and later the *Cariboo Fly*, took surplus farm goods such as butter and eggs on commission or bought them to resell on his own. Island youths shot grouse and ducks to sell to the steamers "as is" (unplucked) for 25¢ each.

John Hepburn settled at Fulford in 1911 to begin a barge service to Victoria. Powering his scow with a car engine, he carried two or three autos. To get speed up, Hepburn would sometimes hitch the engines of the cars he was carrying to his barge engine. He took produce from his farm to the market in Victoria every Saturday.

Later a small launch, the *Elf*, began service on the nine-mile run from Fulford to Sidney. Other little powerboats provided a rudimentary ferry service in this period, stopping at points along the shoreline to pick up passengers who had flagged them down from a rowboat or canoe.

In 1883 Captain John Irving was responsible for merging a number of small shipping firms into the Canadian Pacific Navigation Company. The company's primary goal was to end profit-sapping competition on the Victoria-New Westminster run. Irving became general manager and directors included his brother-in-law, Victoria and San Francisco businessman R.P. Rithet, and the coal magnate Robert Dunsmuir. Majority financial control was held by the Hudson's Bay Company. "Big business had at last invaded a field which had long belonged to rugged individualists. A new era had begun."[3]

Irving's firm dominated the coastal steamship business for the next 18 years, until its purchase by the Canadian Pacific Railway. The first vessels included the sidewheelers *Enterprise, Princess Louise, Maude, Amelia* and *Yosemite,* the sternwheeler *R.P. Rithet* and the old H.B.C. steamer *Otter,* the first propeller-driven ship on the coast when she arrived in 1853.

The little 175-ton *Maude,* converted in 1885 to a propeller steamer, left Victoria twice a week, calling at Nanaimo, Denman Island and Comox. The Denman passengers were put off on a raft and rowed to shore. The *R.P. Rithet* made stops at Miners Bay on Mayne Island and Port Washington on Pender on her summers-only run between Victoria and New Westminster. In the winter the *Enterprise* stopped in midstream in Active Pass every two weeks to drop off mail to a small boat. Sternwheelers were barred by federal marine regulations from crossing the Strait of Georgia in the winter because they were considered less seaworthy than sidewheelers.

The *R.P. Rithet* was one of the finest locally built boats in the area when she was launched in Victoria in 1882. Designed to take miners on a direct voyage from Victoria to Yale on the Fraser River, she was the first steamer in this area with hydraulic steering gear. A reporter for *The British Columbian* of New Westminster gushed at her arrival: "Perfect in lines and model, she is finished in every respect in first class style. The carving in the saloons is elaborate and ornate, while the upholstering, gilding and general finish are simply gorgeous. The staterooms are spacious and convenient, provided with luxurious spring beds and fittings."[4]

The 312-foot *Yosemite,* sleek and fast, had been built in California for service on the Sacramento River. She handled the strait crossing in the winter for the next 22 years. Small boats came out from Gulf Island settlements to take off the mail.

The stumpy old *Otter* went to the scrapyard in 1890. Ten years later the C.P.N. built a new *Otter*, which also served some of the islands. Although more spacious and comfortable than her predecessor, with an elegant dining-room, the new *Otter* was almost as slow as the original. Leaving Victoria at eight A.M., she would take all day to reach Ganges, where there would be an overnight stay. Galiano was not reached until nine or ten the following morning. Nevertheless, the *Otter* was mourned by Galiano residents at a ceremony marking her final call in the spring of 1931. She was sold to the Gibson brothers and became a logging-camp workboat on the west coast of Vancouver Island.

Ferry service to the islands was curtailed in 1886 when the Esquimalt & Nanaimo Railway was completed, and again in 1894 after the Victoria-Sidney railroad, the "Cordwood Express," went into operation. Residents of Salt Spring began taking their small boats to Chemainus or Maple Bay near Duncan to catch the train north or south. Pender and Saturna islanders went to Sidney for the train.

Three small vessels which saw occasional Gulf Islands service were the *Mary Hare, Belcarra* and *Merry Widow*. The *Mary Hare* was on the Sidney-to-Nanaimo route under her owner, Captain Mike Hare. She also made a few stops at the first wharf built in Georgeson Bay on Galiano in 1900. The currents of Active Pass proved too strong for docking, however, and the wharf was abandoned for a new one at Sturdies Bay.

The main service to the islands was provided by the E.&N. Robert Dunsmuir was in the steamship business as well as railroads and coal mines. He acquired the *City of Nanaimo* in 1896 by foreclosing on a mortgage taken out by Captain William Rogers of Vancouver, a onetime friend of the aggressive Scottish financier. He also operated the *Robert Dunsmuir*, known as the "Dirty Bob" to Nanaimo residents because she carried coal cargoes as well as passengers.

Earlier, Dunsmuir had bought the *Thistle* and the *Amelia*, which he had overhauled into a passenger-and-freight vessel, for service along the east coast of Vancouver Island, with stops among the is-

The steamer Joan. (COURTESY BC ARCHIVES)

lands. They were followed in 1892 by the *Joan* (pronounced "Jo-Ann"), which he named after his wife, the former Joanna "Joan" White. This little steamer became a regular caller at Gulf Island ports, running a weekly service between Victoria and Nanaimo. She was the first "car ferry" on the run, carrying two autos lashed to the foredeck and a few below as early as 1907. The *Joan* was also the first steamship to make calls at Saturna Island after a wharf was built at Saturna Beach. At low tides the deeper-draft *R.P. Rithet* was unable to tie up at the wharf and a small fleet of rowboats went out to take off baggage and passengers after the horn-blast announcing her arrival.

The *Joan* was also one of the first steamships to serve the northern Gulf Islands. (The first was the old H.B.C. vessel *Beaver*, which would stop off Denman while the early settlers paddled out on a raft to get supplies.) To make the short voyage from Denman Island to Courtenay, islanders boarded the *Joan* in the afternoon and made two calls at Union Bay, the second at a wharf where freight for Cumberland was unloaded. The steamer then headed north toward

Comox, with the passengers taking dinner on board and a state-room for the night. They got to Courtenay the following morning by horse and buggy from Comox. Other ferries calling at Denman on their way from Nanaimo to Comox included the *City of Nanaimo* and the *Thistle*, while the *Queen City* came from Vancouver.

All these vessels ended up eventually in the hands of the C.P.R., which bought into the C.P.N. in 1901 and completed the purchase two years later. After another two years, in 1905, the C.P.R. also bought the E.&N. railway from Robert Dunsmuir, as well as his little fleet of ships. Included in the C.P.R. purchase were 14 aging vessels, among them the *Charmer*, acquired by Irving in the U.S. in 1887 as the *Premier*. Described then as a "floating palace" when she docked at Vancouver ablaze with electrical lights, she was renamed *Charmer* after being salvaged and repaired following an 1892 mishap in Puget Sound.

The flagship of the C.P.N. fleet had been the *Islander*, a 1,500-ton steel, twin-screw steamer built on the Clyde in 1888. She was a palatial vessel, the only one living up to the "floating palace" label that newspapers trotted out for each new arrival before the turn of the century. The *Islander* saw some service in the Gulf Islands as a C.P.N. vessel; she was lost with 42 lives near Juneau on a tourist cruise in August of 1901 before the transfer to the C.P.R. had been completed.

The *Iroquois* served on the run between Sidney, Nanaimo and the islands six days a week for the first decade of the century before her tragic sinking. Owned by Thomas W. Paterson, she was launched in 1900 to carry the mail from Sidney to the Gulf Islands. She was an ungainly, top-heavy little vessel of 195 tons, which rolled severely in heavy seas and wind. Later, it was revealed that on Paterson's orders, three feet had been added to the width of her upper deck. She sank in a gale on April 10, 1911, just after leaving the Sidney wharf; 15 passengers and six crewmen were drowned, and there were 11 survivors.

On the Victoria-Nanaimo-Comox run, the *Charmer* called four times a week at Denman. One of the few car-carrying vessels in the C.P.R. fleet, she saw service in the southern Gulf Islands, replacing the little wooden steamer *Island Princess* when the latter vessel became too small for the expanding business in 1918. By 1922 the *Charmer* had become the oldest passenger craft on the B.C. coast. She ended her days as a floating hotel at Newcastle Island off Nanaimo in the 1930s. The *Island Princess* was sold to the Gulf Islands Ferry Company in 1930, fitted with diesel engines and renamed the *Cy Peck*.

In 1910 the C.P.R. added the *Princess Mary* to its coastal fleet. The *Mary* was a plodder, but with staterooms and a gracious dining-room, she became one of the most popular vessels on the Gulf Islands-Powell River service, making tri-weekly sailings to Denman, Hornby and Texada on her way across the strait to Powell River. In the 1920s the *Mary* also provided a connection between the Gulf Islands and Vancouver. After she was taken out of service in 1951, her deckhouse became a well-known Victoria restaurant bearing the ship's name.

The first local ferry service in the northern Gulf Islands was primitive. Brothers Irvine and Fred Piercy ran a scow-like craft, which could carry one car, between Denman and Buckley Bay. For power they jacked up a Model-T Ford, started the engine, and then with

The steamer Iroquois *in the Pender canal.* (COURTESY BC ARCHIVES)

the wheels spinning lowered it onto a treadmill which powered the propeller shaft. The next ferryman was Alby Graham, who built a barge to carry cars to the beach near Buckley Bay.

The Denman Islanders petitioned the government for something better. In 1930 Victoria gave a subsidy to Sandy Swan to operate the tug *Garry Point II*, with a scow lashed alongside, to a cement ramp at Buckley Bay. The scow was able to carry three vehicles. Swan held the contract until 1935 when the Baikie family took over. The Baikies borrowed $5,000 to put a new engine in their old logging workboat, the *Moniker*, and added a scow. William Baikie worked on the little ferry as purser and deckhand, and got his mate's ticket. He was studying for a captain's ticket when he died in 1941 at the age of 76. "If we didn't do much profit wise, we did make a happy life for our dad the last years of his life," said son Wallace. Later, a new ferry was built for the Baikie boys which they named the *Billy B.* after their father and with which they held the contract for 17 years. The skipper was Jack Bradley.[5]

Ferry service has always been one of the most controversial topics on the islands, but nowhere more than on Hornby. Before the first government wharf was built in the 1890s near Shingle Spit, the early settlers rowed passengers and freight out to the steamers which anchored offshore. In later years, Hornby was served by both the C.P.R. and Union Steamships. Farm produce went first to Nanaimo on the *Charmer, City of Nanaimo, Princess Mary* and *Joan*. When the Union Steamships' *Cowichan* began calling, the farmers switched to markets in Vancouver and Courtenay.

The *Joan*, with its pleasant bar where thirsty islanders could get a quick drink or even a surreptitious bottle, was always a welcome visitor. Except for the clergy, of course. In 1893 *The Cumberland Weekly News* carried a despatch from its Hornby correspondent: "The Reverend Mr. (Ebenezer) Robson was over last Sunday, showing the way to eternal happiness. But some here, sad to say, appeared to be more interested in getting at the bar of the *Joan* than in getting into church."

One Hornby family associated with the ferry business for 45 years was that of Leon Savoie. This pioneer family of 11, which moved from Denman to Hornby in 1921, started by building boats, and in

1923 began running their little gas-boat *Lipgigg* to the mouth of the Courtenay River twice a week. The trip took 2 1/2 hours each way, carrying farm produce there and feed coming back, as well as passengers both ways. In 1929 she was replaced by the diesel-powered *Water Lily*. Leon's sons Albert and Leo were in charge.

When Denman got the ferry connection with the *Garry Point II* to Buckley Bay in 1930, Hornby Islanders kept their cars on the east side of Denman and crossed Lambert Channel in small boats. It took another 25 years of campaigning to get a ferry from Denman to Hornby. In the meantime the C.P.R. had dropped its run up the east coast of Vancouver Island. A credit union helped finance Albert Savoie to build the first little subsidized barge-ferry in 1955 between the two islands. It took two cars per trip. Because of the lack of a good landing spot, there were many delays caused by low tides in summer, the busiest period.

The prototype of the modern car ferry was the *Motor Princess*, the first diesel-powered vessel built for the C.P.R.. Completed in just three months at Yarrows Shipyard in Victoria in 1923, she was built to carry about seven autos between Sidney and Bellingham. The ungainly little vessel was scorned by ship buffs as the "Galloping Dishpan." There were already 23 similarly designed ferries in Puget Sound, but for B.C. "the age of the squat, fat, fulsome auto ferry had come" and if the C.P.R. had built "more tubby Princesses in the twenties and thirties and fewer sleek, pretty yacht-shaped steamers, there might be a vast profitable Canadian Pacific Railway coastal fleet still in full swing today."[6]

It was not only the purists who were unhappy with the *Motor Princess* and some of its successors; passengers often hated them too. The fit was so tight on some that air had to be let out of tires to get the cars aboard. Windshields were sometimes removed to avoid damage. There were frequent complaints about fumes from the early diesel engines, which, combined with the lurching, rolling motion of these flat-bottomed craft in rough water, caused many queasy stomachs.

The *Motor Princess* ran from Sidney to Steveston for 20 years starting in 1929. During the '30s she ferried week-enders to and from Galiano and the other islands. In 1955 she was sold to the Gulf

Islands Ferry Company and remodelled at the Victoria Machinery Depot shipyard to carry 40 automobiles. Steel upperworks were added over the open, wooden, car deck and a new name, the *Pender Queen*, was bestowed. (The *Motor Princess* had been taken out of service by the C.P.R. in 1950 after new regulations banned wooden superstructures as a fire hazard.) The *Pender Queen* now joined the *Queen of the Islands, Cy Peck, George S. Pearson* and *Salt Spring Queen* on the various islands runs. Her first was between Swartz Bay and Fulford Harbour, replacing the *Cy Peck*, which began serving Galiano, Mayne, Pender and Saturna.

The Gulf Islands Ferry Company was restructured in 1951, with Gavin Mouat of Salt Spring taking over as president. Mouat had begun in the islands transportation business with the little vessel *Ganges*, which operated as a freighter. There were 30 shareholders in the reorganized company. Captain George Maude of the Mayne Island family was vice-president and Des Crofton and Charles Horel were directors. The *Cy Peck* was bought for the Sidney-Fulford run and the *George S. Pearson* sailed between Crofton and Vesuvius.

As C.P.R. service to the islands declined, both Oswald "Sparkie" New of Coast Ferries Ltd. of Vancouver and Mouat's Gulf Islands Ferry Company offered to fill in the gaps. The C.P.R. was reluctant to give up the route altogether and added the *Princess of Alberni*, but soon abandoned the service. Coast Ferries chartered the onetime Union Steamships vessel *Lady Rose* from Harbour Navigation Company in 1955 for a new service between Vancouver and the islands. In 1958 Sparkie New formed the Gulf Islands Navigation Company, replacing Coast Ferries Ltd., to operate a larger new *Island Princess* to replace the *Lady Rose*.

Two years later the government, at the urging of island residents, moved into the ferry business. It took over the Gulf Islands Ferry Company in the summer of 1961 and the new era of the B.C. Ferry Corporation began.

The government had previously been involved in the islands ferry service through subsidies to private operators and, starting in 1954, Department of Highways vessels. Previously restricted to lakes and rivers in the interior, the department began on the coast with the *Catherine Graham* between Denman Island and Buckley Bay; she had a capacity of eight cars and 40 passengers. In 1959 it put the *Ethel Hunter* on a run between Chemainus and Thetis and Kuper islands, the first since the C.P.R. stopped calling at Thetis in the 1920s. Two years later the department took over the Nanaimo-Gabriola run.

Complaints about inadequate ferry service have been one of the constants of Gulf Islands' history. The steady growth of population, accelerated in recent decades, put pressure on the private firms supplying service in the early days, and the government ferry service in the last 30 years. The type of service required has also changed over the years. The early settlers wanted to get their farm produce off the islands to markets on Vancouver Island and the mainland as quickly as possible. Now almost all the food and goods are imported onto the islands by truck on the large new vehicle ferries. The majority of travellers to and from the islands now take their vehicles with them, although passenger-only vessels may make a comeback as transportation patterns change.

Some Gulf Island Place Names

The term "Gulf Islands" is actually a misnomer. Captain George Vancouver in 1792 named the body of water between Vancouver Island and the mainland the "Gulf of Georgia" in the mistaken belief that it was an enclosed inland sea. He chose the name to honour King George III. It was not changed to Strait of Georgia until 1865 when Captain George Henry Richards, the first hydrographer of the area, applied the proper term. It is still commonly called "The Gulf," however, and the term "Gulf Islands" has also stuck. Most of the names here were bestowed in the period 1856 to 1863 by Captain Richards, who surveyed the strait in the Royal Navy vessels *Plumper* and *Hecate*. Richards later became Hydrographer of the Navy in London.

* * *

ACTIVE PASS: Separating Mayne and Galiano Islands, named after the paddle steamer *Active*, an American Revenue and survey vessel which was the first naval ship to make use of the passage, in 1855. It had first been named Plumper Pass by Captain Richards in 1858 after his survey vessel, but Richards graciously acceded to the American claim. The name Plumper Pass continued to be used by locals for some years, and by the Mayne Island post office until 1900.

BAYNES SOUND: Between Denman and Vancouver Islands. Admiral Sir Robert Lambert Baynes, commander-in-chief at Esquimalt, 1857-1860.

BEDWELL HARBOUR, Pender Island: Edward Parker Bedwell, second master of the survey vessel H.M.S. *Plumper* from 1857 to 1860 and master of H.M.S. *Hecate*, 1861-62.

BLUNDEN POINT, South Pender Island: Edward Raynor Blunden, master's assistant of the survey vessel H.M.S. *Hecate* in 1861.

BROWNING HARBOUR, Pender Island: George Alexander Browning, second master of H.M.S. *Hecate*, 1861-62.

BURGOYNE BAY, Salt Spring Island: Captain Hugh Talbot Burgoyne, V.C., of H.M.S. *Ganges*.

D'ARCY ISLAND: Lieutenant John D'Arcy of H.M.S. *Herald*, on survey work in 1846.

DE COURCY ISLAND: Captain Michael De Courcy of the screw corvette, H.M.S. *Pylades*, on this coast in 1859-60.

DENMAN ISLAND: Rear Admiral Joseph Denman, commander-in-chief of Pacific Station, 1864-66.

DESCANSO BAY, Gabriola Island: Called Cala del Descanso (Small Bay of Rest) by Spanish explorers on taking shelter from a storm on June 15, 1792.

FULFORD HARBOUR, Salt Spring Island: Captain John Fulford of H.M.S. *Ganges*.

GANGES, Salt Spring Island: H.M.S. *Ganges*, flagship of Rear Admiral Robert L. Baynes, Pacific Station, 1857-60. Built in Bombay in 1821, she was the last Royal Navy battleship commissioned for service outside home waters.

GABRIOLA ISLAND: The southeastern tip was first called Punta de Gaviota (Cape Seagull) by Spanish explorers in 1791, and changed over the years to Gaviola and then Gabriola.

GALIANO ISLAND: Commander Dionisio Alcala Galiano, captain of the Spanish exploring ship *Sutil* which was in the area in 1792.

GEORGINA POINT, Mayne Island: Georgina Mary Seymour, wife of Admiral Sir George F. Seymour, commander-in-chief of the Royal Navy's Pacific Station, 1844-46.

GOWLLAND POINT, South Pender Island: Staff Commander John Thomas Gowlland, second master on H.M.S. *Plumper* and *Hecate*, involved in survey work with Captain George Henry Richards, 1857-62.

HELEN POINT, Mayne Island: Helen McKay, wife of Chief Trader Joseph W. McKay of the Hudson's Bay Company.

HOPE BAY, North Pender Island: Rutherford Hope, one of the island's first two settlers.

HORNBY ISLAND: Admiral Phipps Hornby, commander of Pacific Station, 1847-1851. Hornby had served as a junior officer on Nelson's flagship *Victory*. Geoffrey Mountain on Hornby Island is named after his son, Geoffrey Thomas Phipps Hornby, who served as flag lieutenant under his father on the station and later became an admiral himself.

HORTON BAY, Mayne Island: Robert John Horton, a Hudson's Bay Company official at Victoria who assisted with marine surveys on the *Otter*.

JAMES ISLAND: Sir James Douglas, head of the Hudson's Bay Company on this coast and later governor of the colony of British Columbia.

KUPER ISLAND: Augustus Leopold Kuper, captain of H.M.S. *Thetis* stationed at Esquimalt, 1851-53, and later admiral.

LAMBERT CHANNEL: Separates Denman and Hornby Islands. Lionel Lambert, flag lieutenant to Rear Admiral Robert L. Baynes of the flagship H.M.S. *Ganges*.

LASQUETI ISLAND: Juan Maria Lasqueti, a prominent Spanish naval officer, honoured by Jose Maria Narvaez, who explored the Strait of Georgia in 1791 as commander of the *Saturnina*.

LYALL HARBOUR, Saturna Island: David Lyall, surgeon aboard

the survey vessel H.M.S. *Plumper*, 1858-59.

MAYNE ISLAND: Richard Charles Mayne, lieutenant on the survey vessel H.M.S. *Plumper* on this coast 1857-61, later promoted to admiral. Author of *Four Years in British Columbia and Vancouver Island*, published in 1862.

MINERS BAY, Mayne Island: Named after miners who camped in Active Pass *en route* from Victoria to the Fraser River gold rush.

MORESBY ISLAND: Rear Admiral Fairfax Moresby, commander-in-chief, Pacific Station, 1850-53. (Also Moresby Island in Queen Charlotte group.)

ORLEBAR POINT, Gabriola Island: Lieutenant V.B. Orlebar, commander of gunboat H.M.S. *Rocket* on this coast 1875-82.

PENDER ISLAND: Daniel Pender, second master of H.M.S. *Plumper* and master, H.M.S. *Hecate*, doing survey work on this coast, 1857-70. Later promoted to captain and worked at Royal Navy's hydrographic office in London.

PIERS ISLAND: Henry Piers, surgeon aboard H.M.S. *Satellite* on this coast 1857-60.

PORLIER PASS: Between Galiano and Valdes Islands. Antonio Porlier, a Spanish official in Madrid.

PORT WASHINGTON, Pender Island: Washington Grimmer was the island's first postmaster at this cove on the west side. Grimmer's father James, an Englishman, had visited the U.S. where he became an admirer of George Washington.

PORTLAND ISLAND: H.M.S. *Portland* was the flagship of Rear Admiral Fairfax Moresby. The island became Princess Margaret Marine Park in 1958 but both names are used.

PREEDY HARBOUR, Thetis Island: Admiral George William Preedy, lieutenant aboard H.M.S. *Constance* on this coast 1846-49.

PREVOST ISLAND: Captain James C. Prevost of H.M.S. *Satellite* on west coast 1857-60. Married to daughter of Admiral Moresby, was a member of San Juan Boundary Commission, and later promoted to admiral.

REID ISLAND: James Murray Reid, captain of the H.B.C.'s brigantine *Vancouver* and later with the company in Victoria.

SALT SPRING ISLAND: First known as "Chu-an," a Cowichan

Indian name meaning "facing the sea." It was soon Anglicized to "Tuan," and later to "Tuam," after a town in Ireland. Then a group of H.B.C. officers who planned to exploit the 14 salt springs on the northern end of the island began calling it Saltspring Island. In 1859 Captain George Richards further confused the issue by naming it "Admiral Island" after Rear Admiral Robert L. Baynes, commander-in-chief at Esquimalt. Richards's choice didn't last long, however, and by 1880 charts and maps bore the name Salt Spring Island. That was not the end of the matter, however. The Geographic Board of Canada favours single-barrelled names and in 1924 changed the name once again to Saltspring. Since that time it has been either one or two words, depending on preference.

SAMUEL ISLAND: Samuel Campbell, assistant surgeon on H.M.S. *Plumper*, later fleet surgeon. Campbell Bay on Mayne Island is also named after him.

SANSUM NARROWS: Between Salt Spring and Vancouver Islands. Lieutenant Arthur Sansum of H.M.S. *Thetis*, under Captain A.L. Kuper.

SATELLITE CHANNEL: H.M.S. *Satellite*, a 21-gun screw corvette which was on this coast from 1857 to 1860 under Captain James C. Prevost.

SATURNA ISLAND: The Spanish naval schooner *Saturnina*, which explored the Strait of Georgia in 1791.

SCOTT POINT, Salt Spring Island: William Ernest Scott, member of the B.C. Board of Horticulture who lived on Fruitvale Ranch nearby around the turn of the century.

SOUTHEY POINT, Salt Spring Island: James L. Southey, secretary to Rear Admiral Robert L. Baynes of Pacific Station.

TEXADA ISLAND: Felix de Tejada (Texada), a rear admiral in the Spanish navy.

THETIS ISLAND: Frigate H.M.S. *Thetis*, on this coast 1851-53.

TRIBUNE BAY, Hornby Island: H.M.S. *Tribune*, under Captain Geoffrey Thomas Phipps Hornby.

TRINCOMALI CHANNEL: Sailing frigate H.M.S. *Trincomalee*, on Pacific Station, 1852-56, and named after the port of the same name in the Indian Ocean. She was built in Bombay in 1817.

TUMBO ISLAND: Named Tumbow by Commander Charles Wilkes of the U.S. Navy in 1841. Captain Richards later asserted British sovereignty over the island by changing the name to Tumbo, a Spanish word meaning "fall", to imply that it had been so named by the early Spanish explorers before Wilkes.

VALDES ISLAND: Captain Cayetano Valdes of the Spanish navy, commander of exploring vessel *Mexicana* in 1792.

VAN ANDA, Texada Island: Van Anda Blewett, the son of Ed Blewett, founder of the Van Anda Copper and Gold Company. Blewett Sr. chose the name of a famed New York newspaperman in the late 1800s, Carr Van Anda.

VESUVIUS BAY, Salt Spring Island: The paddle sloop H.M.S. *Vesuvius*, which served in the Black Sea during the Crimean War.

VIRAGO POINT, Galiano Island: The paddle sloop-of-war H.M.S. *Virago*, on this coast in 1854.

WALKER HOOK, Salt Spring Island: Edward Walker, pioneer resident of Nanaimo and in marine service of H.B.C.

(Sources: *British Columbia Coast Names*, by Captain John T. Walbran; *Place Names of the Pacific Northwest Coast*, by Lynn Middleton; *British Columbia Place Names*, by G.P.V. and Helen B. Akrigg; *San Juan Island: Coastal Place Names and Cartographic Nomenclature*, by Bryce Wood; and *Salt Spring Island*, by Bea Hamilton.)

Footnotes

THE PEOPLE

1. Elliott. *Mayne Island*, p. 7.
2. Filberg, R.J. *The Truck Logger*, January 1968, quoted in Baikie, *Rolling with the Times*.
3. Baikie. *Rolling with the Times*, p. 27.
4. Hayman. *Robert Brown and the Vancouver Island Exploring Expedition*, p. 122.
5. Wilson. *Diary.* (*Times Past*, p. 70.); Baikie, p. 76.
6. Dora Payne. British Columbia Archives and Records Service, Transcript, Audio Tape 807-1.
7. Robert Roe. Tape 787-1.
8. *A Gulf Islands Patchwork*, p. 89.

MAYNE

1. Mary Backlund. Tape 792-1.
2. Elliott. *Mayne Island*, p. 6-7.
3. Nelson. "Silva Family." Typescript.

4. Graham. *Lights of the Inside Passage*, p. 14.
5. Borradaile. *Lady of Culzean*, p. 25.
6. Captain and Mrs. George A. Maude. Tape 790-1.
7. Borradaile. *Lady of Culzean*. p. 2, 3 (and preceding quote).
8. Hamilton. *Western Shores*, p. 67-70.
9. Borradaile. *Lady of Culzean*, p. 4.
10. J.K. Nesbitt. *Vancouver Sun*, June 23, 1971.
11. *Mayne Island Fall Fair Booklet*, p. 9.
12. Borradaile. *Lady of Culzean*, p. 1.
13. Elliott. *Mayne Island*, p. 49, 52.
14. *Fall Fair Booklet*, p. 4, 5.
15. Elliott. *Mayne Island*, p. 65.
16. Swartz papers. BCARS. Box 15. File 17.

GALIANO
1. Archie Georgeson. Tape 793-1.
2. Walter. *Early Days Among the Gulf Islands of British Columbia*, p. 6-9.
3. *Colonist*, November 26, 1978, p. 5. (Letter to editor).
4. Elliott. "Galiano Island Pioneer." *The Beaver*.
5. Interview by author with Ruth (Enke) Chambers at her home in Saanich, 1990.
6. Graham. *Lights of the Inside Passage*, p. 81; Devina Baines, Tape 795-1.
7. Baines, *Ibid*.
8. Mrs. Frances (Allison) Brown. Tape 797-1.
9. Mr. and Mrs. Crawford Twiss. Tape 794-1.

SATURNA
1. *Colonist*, January 16, 1886, p. 3; and October 18, 1889, p. 4 (advertisement).
2. Winifred Grey "Excerpts from Memoirs"; and Constance Grey Swartz, Tape 783-l.
3. *A Gulf Islands Patchwork*, p. 52.
4. Mrs. Dorothy (Payne) Richardson. Tape 806-1; Mrs. Geraldine (Payne) Hulbert. Tape 808-1.; Constance Swartz. Tape 783-1.
5. Hulbert, *Ibid*.
6. Walbran, *British Columbia Coast Names*, p. 431-32.
7. *Vancouver Island Pilot*. 1861.
8. Graham. *Lights of the Inside Passage*, p. 24.
9. Mrs. Peter Georgeson. Tape 805-1.
10. Takata. *Nikkei Legacy*, p. 78, 79.
11. Elliott. *Mayne Island*, p. 20-21; Vancouver *Province*, November 4, 1903, p. 7.

Footnotes

12. Swartz papers. Box 17, File 22.
13. *Western Living.* June, 1990. p. 92.

PENDER
1. Tolmie. "Harbours and Anchorages in the Haro Strait and Gulf of Georgia."
2. Mr. and Mrs. Herbert Spalding. Tape 784-1.
3. "Notes on Pender Island in Early Days," p. 1.
4. Neptune Grimmer. Tape 786-1.
5. *Ibid; A Gulf Islands Patchwork,* p. 20-21.
6. *Ibid,* p. 22-23.
7. "Notes on Pender Island in Early Days," p. 2.
8. Mary Hamilton. Tape 810-1.
9. Borradaile. *Lady of Culzean,* p. 44-46.
10. Hamilton. Tape 810-1.
11. Victor Menzies. Tape 789-1; "Albert Hugh Menzies and Valley Home Farm, Pender Island." Typescript.
12. Boucher. Typescript.
13. Swartz papers.
14. Mrs. Beatrice (Spalding) Freeman. Tape 785-1.
15. Hamilton. Tape 810-1.
16. Swartz. Tape 783-1.
17. Sweet. *Islands in Trust,* p. 159.

MORESBY, PORTLAND, PIERS
1. Len A. Bittancourt. Tape 798-1.
2. Richardson. *Pig War Islands,* p. 271-73.
3. "Notes on Pender Island in Early Days," p. 4.
4. Richardson. *Pig War Islands,* p. 273.
5. Robert Roe. Tape 787-1.
6. Dunae. *Gentlemen Emigrants,* p. 115-117.

SALT SPRING
1. Roberts. *Salt Spring Saga,* p. 10-11.
3. Pilton. Thesis, p. 142.
3. Mrs. Mabel Davis. Tape 800-2.
4. Bea Hamilton. *Salt Spring Island,* p. 18; Reverend Ebenezer Robson, Diary.
5. Walbran. *British Columbia Coast Names,* p. 12.
6. *New Westminster Times.* December 10, 1859, p. 1.
7. Flucke. A.F. "Early Days on Saltspring Island." p. 170-71, 180.
8. Killian. *Go Do Some Great Thing,* p. 109.
9. Wallace (Stark). Typescript; Pilton, p. 142-144; Killian, p. 104-105.

10. Robson. Diary.
11. Bowen. *Three Dollar Dreams*, p. 361-63.
12. *Times Past*, p. 6-7
13. Green. "Diary of Salt Spring Survey."
14. *Times Past*, p. 12.
15. Mrs. Margaret Cunningham. Tape 799-1; *Times Past*, p. 41-43.
16. Flucke, p. 193.
17. Nanaimo *Free Press*, June. 1892.
18. Wilson. Diary.
19. Wilson. *Parish and Home*.
20. Des Crofton. Tape 100-1.
21. Mrs. Beryl Weatherell. Tape 796-1; Wilson. *Parish and Home*.
22. Cartwright. *A Late Summer*, p. 10.
23. Adachi. *The Enemy That Never Was*, p. 333-34 and p. 407 (footnote 63).

THETIS, KUPER
1. Gustafson, Elliott. *Memories of the Chemainus Valley*, p. 12.
2. Dunae. *Gentlemen Emigrants*, p. 111.
3. Olsen. *Water Over the Wheel*, p. 84.
4. Roberts. Diary.

GABRIOLA, VALDES
1. Lewis-Harrison. *The People of Gabriola*, p. 71.
2. Bowen. *Three Dollar Dreams*, p. 164-65.
3. Graham. *Keepers of the Light*, p. 102-05.
4. Rhodes. "Gabriola Island." Typescript.
5. Ovanin. *Island Heritage Buildings*, p. 39.
6. Lillard. *The Brother XII: The Devil of DeCourcy Island*; Loomis. *Small Stories of a Gentle Island*, p. 27-34; Cummings. *Gunkholing in the Gulf Islands*, p. 192-198.

LASQUETI, TEXADA
1. Mason. *Lasqueti Island: History and Memory*, p. 2-3.
2. Sweet. *Islands in Trust*, p. 139.
3. Graham. *Lights of the Inside Passage*, p. 56.
4. Rushton. *Whistle Up the Inlet*, p. 158.
5. May. *Texada*, p. xi.
6. Guppy. *Wetcoast Ventures*, p. 18.
7. Quoted by Peter Corley-Smith in *Barnstorming to Bush Flying, 1910-1930*, p. 164. Sono Nis Press. Victoria. 1989.
8. Rushton, p. 67-69.

DENMAN, HORNBY

1. *Women's Institute Pamphlet.*
2. Dean. "The Early History of Denman Island. . . ."
3. Isbister. *My Ain Folk*, p. 15.
4. Buckham. Papers.
5. *Land of Plenty*, p. 139.
6. Graham. *Lights of the Inside Passage*, p. 30-31.
7. MacKay. *The Lumberjacks*, p. 160.
8. Baikie. *Rolling with the Times*, p. 12-20.
9. Smith, Gerow. *Hornby Island*, p. 3; Ovanin. *Island Heritage Buildings*, p. 23.
10. Corrigal. *Historic Hornby Island*, p. 17-18.
11. Smith, Gerow. *Hornby Island*, p. 28; *Oxford English Dictionary*.
12. Baikie. *Rolling with the Times*, p. 23.
13. *Ibid*, p. 24.
14. Smith, Gerow. *Hornby Island.* p. 27, 30.

THE BOATS

1. Wilson. Diary.
2. Borradaile. *Lady of Culzean*, p. 42.
3. Hacking. "British Columbia Steamboat Days, 1870-1883," p. 100.
4. *The British Columbian*, June 14, 1882. (Quoted in *ibid.*)
5. Baikie. *Rolling with the Times*, p. 105.
6. Greene. *Personality Ships*, p. 246.

Bibliography

BOOKS

Adachi, Ken. *The Enemy That Never Was: A History of the Japanese Canadians*. McClelland & Stewart. Toronto. 1976.

A Gulf Islands Patchwork: Some Early Events on the Islands of Galiano, Mayne, Saturna, North and South Pender. Gulf Islands Branch, B.C. Historical Association. 1961.

Baikie, Wallace. *Rolling with the Times*. Campbell River. 1985.

Borradaile, John. *Lady of Culzean: Mayne Island*. Private Printing. Second edition, 1971.

Bowen, Lynne. *Three Dollar Dreams*. Oolichan Books. Lantzville, B.C. 1987.

Cartwright, E.R. *A Late Summer: Memoirs*. Caravel Press. London. 1964.

Corrigal, Margery. *Historic Hornby Island.* Comox District Free Press. Courtenay. 1978.

Cummings, Al, and Bailey-Cummings, Jo. *Gunkholing in the Gulf Islands.* Nor-Westing. Edmonds, Washington. 1986.

Dunae, Patrick A. *Gentlemen Emigrants.* Douglas & McIntyre. Vancouver. 1981.

Elliott, Marie. *Mayne Island.* Gulf Islands Press. Mayne Island. 1984.

Gough, Barry. *Gunboat Frontier: British Maritime Authority and Northwest Coast Indians, 1846-90.* University of British Columbia Press. Vancouver. 1984.

Graham, Donald. *Keepers of the Light.* Harbour Publishing. Madeira Park, B.C. 1985.

—— *Lights of the Inside Passage.* Harbour Publishing. Madeira Park, B.C. 1986.

Greene, Ruth. *Personality Ships of British Columbia.* Marine Tapestry Publications. West Vancouver. 1969.

Guppy, Walter. *Wetcoast Ventures: Mine-Finding on Vancouver Island.* Cappis Press. Victoria. 1988.

Gustafson, Lillian, and Elliott, Gordon, editors. *Memories of the Chemainus Valley.* Chemainus Valley Historical Society. 1978.

Hacking, Norman, and W. Kaye Lamb. *The Princess Story: A Century and a Half of West Coast Shipping.* Mitchell Press. Vancouver. 1974.

Hamilton, Bea. *Salt Spring Island.* Mitchell Press. Vancouver. 1969.

Hamilton, James H. *Western Shores: Narratives of the Pacific Coast.* Progress Publishing. Vancouver. 1932.

Hayman, John, editor. *Robert Brown and the Vancouver Island Exploring Expedition.* University of British Columbia Press. Vancouver. 1989.

Hearn, George and Wilkie, David. *The Cordwood Limited: A History of the Victoria & Sidney Railway.* B.C. Railway Historical Association. Victoria. 1966.

Isbister, Winnifred. A. *My Ain Folk: Denman Island, 1875-1975.* Courtenay. 1976.

Killian, Crawford. *Go Do Some Great Thing: The Black Pioneers of*

Bibliography

British Columbia. Douglas & McIntyre. Vancouver. 1978.

Land of Plenty: A History of the Comox District. Ptarmigan Press. Campbell River. 1987.

Lewis-Harrison, June. *The People of Gabriola: A History of Our Pioneers*. Gabriola Island, B.C. 1982.

Lillard, Charles. *The Devil of De Courcy Island*. Porcepic Books. Victoria. 1990.

Loomis, Ruth. *Small Stories of A Gentle Island*. Reflections. Ladysmith, B.C. 1986.

MacKay, Donald. *The Lumberjacks*. McGraw-Hill Ryerson. Toronto. 1978.

Mason, Elda Copley. *Lasqueti Island: History and Memory*. South Wellington, B.C. 1976.

May, Mr. and Mrs. Cecil, editors. *Texada*. Centennial Committee. 1960.

Middleton, Lynn. *Place Names of the Pacific Northwest Coast*. Elldee Publishing Company. Victoria. 1969.

Newell, Gordon, editor. *The H.W. McCurdy Marine History of the Pacific Northwest*. Superior Publishing Company. Seattle. 1966.

Obee, Bruce. *The Gulf Islands Explorer*. Whitecap Books. North Vancouver, B.C. Fourth edition. 1988.

Olsen, W.H. *Water Over the Wheel*. Chemainus Valley Historical Association. Chemainus, B.C. 1963.

Ovanin, Thomas K. *Island Heritage Buildings*. Islands Trust. Victoria. 1984.

Reimer, Derek, editor. *The Gulf Islanders*. Sound Heritage, Vol. V, No. 4. Aural History. BCARS. 1976.

Richardson, David. *Pig War Islands*. Orcas Publishing Company. East Sound, Washington. 1971.

Roberts, Eric A. *Salt Spring Saga*. Driftwood. Ganges, B.C. 1962.

Rogers, Fred. *Shipwrecks of British Columbia*. J.J. Douglas. Vancouver. 1973.

Rushton, Gerald A. *Whistle Up the Inlet: The Union Steamship Story*. J.J. Douglas. Vancouver. 1974.

Smith, Elizabeth and Gerow, David. *Hornby Island: The Ebb and Flow*. Ptarmigan Press. Campbell River. 1988.

Sweet, Arthur Fielding. *Islands in Trust*. Oolichan Books. Lantzville, B.C. 1988.

Takata, Toyo. *Nikkei Legacy: The Story of Japanese Canadians from Settlement to Today*. NC Press. Toronto. 1983.

Times Past: Salt Spring Island Houses and History Before the Turn of the Century. Ganges, B.C. 1983.

Toynbee, Richard Mouat. *Snapshots of Early Salt Spring and Other Favoured Islands*. Mouat's Trading Company. Ganges, B.C. 1978.

Turner, Robert D. *The Pacific Princesses*. Sono Nis Press. Victoria. 1977.

Walbran, Captain John T. *British Columbia Coast Names*. The Library's Press - J.J. Douglas. Vancouver. Reprint. 1971.

Walter, Margaret. *Early Days Among the Gulf Islands of British Columbia*. Victoria. 1958.

Wright, E.D. editor. *Lewis and Dryden's Marine History of the Pacific Northwest*. Superior Publishing Company reprint. Seattle. 1967.

ARTICLES

Dickie, Grace. "The Hunter Family of Thetis Island." *B.C. Historical News*. Winter, 1990.

Elliott, Marie. "Galiano Island Pioneer." (Charles Groth). *The Beaver*. Winter 1980, p. 51-54

Grescoe, Audrey. "Paradise in Peril." *Western Living*. June, 1990.

Flucke, A.F. "Early Days on Saltspring Island." *B.C. Historical Quarterly*, July-October, 1951, p. 170-71, 180.

Hacking, Norman. "British Columbia Steamboat Days, 1870-1883." *B.C. Historical Quarterly*. April, 1947.

Hannay, Margaret. "British Columbia Gulf Island Cemeteries." B.C. Genealogical Society. Richmond, B.C. 1989.

Local, regional and city newspapers relevant to the area.

PRINTED PAMPHLETS

Mayne Island Fall Fair. Centennial edition. 1971. BCARS.

Vancouver Island Pilot. 1861. BCARS.
Women's Institute Pamphlet. Denman Island. BCARS.
Wilson, Rev. E.F. *Salt Spring Island.* 1895. BCARS.

UNPUBLISHED PAPERS AND THESES

Boucher, Frank F. "No Englishmen Need Apply." Typescript. BCARS.
Buckham, A.F. Papers. BCARS.
Burkitt, W.A. Typescript. BCARS.
Dean, O.S. "The Early History of Denman Island and its Pioneers." Typescript. BCARS.
Green, Ashdown. "Diary of Salt Spring Survey, June 8 to Nov. 22, 1874."
Grey Papers: Ralph Grey diary; "Excerpts from Memoirs," by Mrs. Ralph Geoffrey Grey, *née* Winifred Grace Spalding Higgs. (Prepared and read by her daughter, Constance Grey Swartz, at meeting of B.C. Historical Association at Port Washington, Pender Island, May 13, 1956.). BCARS.
Groth, Charles. Diary. BCARS.
Irby, Charles C. "Black Settlers on Saltspring Island in the Nineteenth Century". Paper delivered to 35th annual meeting of Association of Pacific Coast Geographers at Hayward, California, June 15, 1972.
Ludwig, C. H. "A Brief History of Waldron Island." BCARS.
Menzies, A.M. "Albert Hugh Menzies and Valley Home Farm, Pender Island." BCARS.
Nelson, Leo and Gaylia. "Silva Family." BCARS.
New, Ida. "History of Galiano Island." Collection of newspaper articles. BCARS.
"Notes on Pender Island in Early Days." Anon. Clippings File. Microfilm reel 110. BCARS.
Pilton, James. W. "Negro Settlement in British Columbia, 1858-1871". Unpublished MA thesis. University of British Columbia. 1951.
Rhodes, W.A. "Gabriola Island." BCARS.
Roberts, Robert J. Diary. BCARS.

Robson, Ebenezer. Diary. BCARS.

Swartz, Constance Grey. Papers. BCARS.

Tolmie, W.F. "Harbours and Anchorages in the Haro Strait and Gulf of Georgia." Memorandum, n.d. BCARS.

Wallace, Marie Albertina Stark. "Recollections of Her Mother Sylvia Stark." Typescript. BCARS.

Wilson, Rev. E.F. Diary. BCARS. (Also reprinted in *Times Past*.) Audio Tapes. BCARS.

Index